بسم الله الرحمن الرحيم

*Selections from the*

# DIWAN

*of*

## Shaykh Salih al-Ja'fari

**VOLUME I**

Imam Ghazali Institute
Light of the Azhar

Copyright © 2021 Light of the Azhar
info@lightoftheazhar.com
www.lightoftheazhar.com
No part of this publication may be reproduced, stored in a retrieval system, or transmitted in any form or by any means, electronic or otherwise, including photocopying, recording, and internet without prior permission of Light of the Azhar.

*ISBN:* 978-1-8384776-5-3

*Title:* Selections from the Diwan of Shaykh Salih al-Jaʿfari—Volume I

*Author:* Shaykh Ṣāliḥ al-Jaʿfarī

*Translation:* Ahmad Ali al-Adani

*Transcription, Proofreading & Editing:*
Mohammed A Shamsudoha and Ahmad Muhammad

*Typesetting & Cover design:*
Shaik Abdul Khafid Mastan, Muhammadan Press

Exclusively distributed by Imam Ghazali Publishing, New Jersey, USA.

Managed by Sattaur Publishing Group.

info@imamghazalipublishing.com
www.imamghazalipublishing.com

# Contents


Introduction 1
Shaykh Ṣāliḥ al-Jaʿfarī 5
1 - The Family of My Beloved, You Are My Cure 11
2 - al-Maqbūla, The Accepted Qaṣīda 17
3 - O Family of Aḥmad 45
4 - Seeker of Good 57
5 - O My Masters! 61
6 - The Light of Allah 77
7 - Messenger of Allah, I Halted My Mount 85
8 - Did It Call You? 91
9 - The Ship of the Folk 97
10 - Drink 107
11 - Welcome! 111
12 - Everyone Withdrew 139
13 - A Pleasant Time 147
14 - Zaynab 159
15 - Lord, By My Love 163
16 - Lord, By the Chosen One 173
17 - God is Pleased 191
18 - Hasten Towards Them 199
19 - O Father of the Resplendent! 205
20 - The Pure Blessings 219

# Introduction

In the Name of Allah, the Beneficent, the Most Merciful. He Who has taught man articulate speech. And blessings and peace be on His messenger, who was sent as a mercy to all of creation, our master Muḥammad, likewise on his purified family, noble companions and those who follow in righteousness till the Day of Judgement.

To proceed:

Our master, the illustrious Imām and erudite scholar of al-Azhar, Shaykh Ṣāliḥ al-Jaʿfarī, authored twelve volumes of poetry dealing with many subjects, ranging from the remembrance and glorification of Allah ﷻ, advice for the one traversing the spiritual path to Allah, exalting the excellence of the Beloved ﷺ and the Ahl al-Bayt عليهم السلام, and the virtues of the Path's litanies and ṣalawāt.

The general breakdown are as follows:

Volumes I and II deal with the relationship between the shaykh and murīd. It also explains the virtues of the Path.

Volumes III to VIII are known as the "Muḥammadiyyāt", focusing on the praise of the excellence of the Messenger of Allah ﷺ and the Ahl al-Bayt عليهم السلام.

Volumes IX to XII are known as the "Ilāhiyyāt", focusing on the Remembrance of Allah extolling the Almighty's Divine Attributes.

Due to the arduous task of rendering large amounts of Arabic poetry into English, we have sufficed ourselves with the aim to present selections from these volumes to create a running series, this book being volume I of the projected series. It should be noted that these selections from the Diwan, were chosen specifically by Shaykh Muḥammad Ṣāliḥ al-Jaʿfarī, the grandson of Shaykh Ṣāliḥ al-Jaʿfarī and the Shaykh of the Jaʿfarīyya Ṭarīqa in Egypt and the Islamic World. The core of these selections, just as the shaykh's poetry overall, will be from the genre of what is known as madīḥ (praise poetry). This series of bilingual (fully-vowelized

Arabic with an easy-to-read English translation) volumes have been designed for use in regular gatherings of remembrance. Under the guidance of Shaykh Muḥammad Ṣāliḥ al-Jaʿfarī and the kind help of renowned scholar and munshid, Shaykh Mustafa al-Shadhili al-Azhari (Egypt), we have specially recorded the audio recitations of these selections from the Diwan in a studio, which can be found on our website and YouTube channel[1].

In his book, *Poetry in Praise of Prophetic Perfection*, Dr. Oludamini Ogunnaike mentions that the genre of madīḥ encompasses at least four different categories: dhikr/ṣalawāt, ḥilya, duʾā, and being.

Dhikr/ṣalawāt: The poems of praise often invoke the names of Allah and call for blessings and salutations on the Prophet ﷺ.

Ḥilya: The poems describe the various physical and spiritual qualities of the Prophet ﷺ and his household.

Duʾā: As with the embedded dhikr, the madīḥ consists of supplications for forgiveness, felicity, succor, etc., in this life and the next.

Being: The reality of these poems are that they are more than mere poems. They are elixirs for the souls. With regular recitation and reflection on their meanings, one is transformed by their lights and secrets.

In this light, Shaykh ʿAbd al-Ghanī al-Jaʿfarī, speaking on the methodology of his father, Shaykh Ṣāliḥ al-Jaʿfarī, says:

> We have discussed in the biography of our Shaykh a subtle point of discussion, which we recognize as the secret to the Jaʿfarī spiritual openings. We have not found a door that our Shaykh preferred, in terms of gifts and spiritual support more than the door of the Prophetic praise (madīḥ). The Jaʿfarī Diwan, which is in numerous volumes, expresses this Lordly opening which he expounds from his very essence, the love for the presence of al-Mustafa ﷺ. The Prophet ﷺ spoke the truth in his saying: "The one who loves a thing mentions it often."
>
> Our Shaykh has taken this path, i.e. longing for the Messenger of Allah ﷺ, for the spiritual upbringing of his students. And from that is found in the introduction to his qaṣīda 'al-Maqbūla': "O lover of the Messenger of

1 For the melodies of the poems, please visit our website: www.lightoftheazhar.com and our YouTube page: https://www.youtube.com/c/LightoftheAzhar

> Allah ﷺ shall I not show you the closest of paths to reach the Messenger of Allah ﷺ without weariness or difficulty? Pay attention! It is in the praise of him ﷺ whether listening to or reciting them, with a sound heart and great love, while imagining him ﷺ in your heart. And this imagining will either be by imagining his noble Rawḍa if you have visited it or bringing to mind his form ﷺ if you have seen him in a dream or based on his description in the Shamā'il. And we behold this at the time of sending prayers and peace upon him ﷺ always."
>
> This door of spiritual openings, which our Shaykh traveled, is a clear opening, and whoever traverses it will arrive, and whoever arrives will be connected, and whoever is connected will see and witness, and whoever has witnessed, has intimate discourse, and becomes acquainted, and whoever becomes acquainted, is guided to the Muḥammadan Reality, thus he multiplies love by love. As he ﷺ has said: "A man is with the one he loves."

This is the core purpose of the madīḥ of Sidna Shaykh Ṣāliḥ al-Jaʿfarī; they are transformative and represent acceptance and invitation to the presence of the Prophet ﷺ and his household. Speaking of this invitation our shaykh, Muḥammad Ṣāliḥ al-Jaʿfarī narrates to us in a counsel:

> I heard Sidna Shaykh ʿAbd al-Ghanī say, "Mawlana Shaykh Ṣāliḥ wrote the qaṣīda 'al-Jaʿfarīyyu lahu fi ḥubbikum ʾamalun' and in it he mentioned Mawlana al-Imām al-Ḥasan and Mawlana al-Imām al-Ḥusayn. When Mawlana Shaykh Ṣāliḥ had gone to sleep, he saw his grandfather, Sayyiduna al-Imām ʿAlī (may Allah ennoble his countenance and be well pleased with him) who said to him: "My son Ṣāliḥ, you mentioned my children but did not mention me?". Upon hearing this, Mawlana Shaykh Ṣāliḥ woke up immediately and wrote some verses as an addition to the qaṣīda."

أُذْكُرْ عَلِيًّا إِذَا مَا جَاءَ مُبْتَدِراً

أَهْلَ العَدَاوَةِ فِي بَدْرٍ بِلَا مَهَلِ

وَ السَّيْفُ يَلْمَعُ فِي يُمْنَاهُ ذُو خَطَرٍ

أَرْدَى الأَعَادِي أُهَيْلَ الرُّمْحِ وَ الأَسَلِ

لَهُ زَبِيرٌ كَمِثْلِ الأَسْدِ فِي أَجَمٍ
يُرْدِي الأَعَادِي بِوَهْمِ الرُّعْبِ وَ الوَجَلِ

Mention ʿAlī when he came rushing
at the people of enmity at Badr, with no delay
And the sword gleamed in his right hand, menacingly
Killing the enemies, the holders of spears and spikes
He has a roar like a lion in the jungle
It takes down enemies with the misgivings of fear and dismay

Sidna Shaykh ʿAbd al-Ghanī said if you recite this qaṣīda regularly and frequently, you will see with ease, Mawlana al-Imām ʿAlī (may Allah ennoble his countenance and be well pleased with him). This qaṣīda can be considered an 'invitation' towards Mawlana al-Imām ʿAlī (may Allah ennoble his countenance and be well pleased with him). Likewise, when one recites the famous qaṣīda 'al-Ghunmu madḥu Rasūlillah yuntadharu'[2], this is an 'invitation' towards Sayyidina ʿUmar b. al-Khattab ﷺ [meaning the reciter will see Sayyidina ʿUmar ﷺ in their dream, by the permission of Allah]."

Again, this shows us that these are not mere poems of a mere poet, but spiritual outpourings of the Muḥammadan inheritance. We ask Allah ﷻ to reward Shaykh Ṣāliḥ with the best reward on our behalf and we ask that He give us success to recite these poems regularly and to benefit us by them in this life and the next.

2 This poem and the others mentioned here will be presented in upcoming volumes of this book series, in shā' Allāh.

# Shaykh Ṣāliḥ al-Ja'farī

## Birth

Shaykh Ṣāliḥ al-Ja'farī ﷺ was born on the 15th Jumāda al-Thānī 1328 AH (24th June 1910 CE) in the town of Dongola, Sudan.[3]

## Noble Lineage

He is the descendant of al-Sayyid 'Alī al-Hādī ﷺ, b. al-Sayyid Muḥammad al-Jawād ﷺ, b. al-Sayyid 'Alī al-Riḍā ﷺ, b. al-Sayyid Mūsā al-Kāẓim ﷺ, b. al-Sayyid Ja'far al-Ṣādiq ﷺ, b. al-Sayyid Muḥammad al-Bāqir ﷺ, b. al-Sayyid al-Imām 'Alī Zayn al-Ābidīn ﷺ, b. Mawlānā al-Imām al-Ḥusayn ﷺ, b. al-Imām 'Alī ﷺ, the husband of the pure lady Sayyida Fāṭima al-Zahrā' ﷺ, the daughter of our Prophet and beloved, Sayyiduna Muḥammad ﷺ.

## Early Life

The Shaykh was brought up in Dongola, where he was raised with a religious and spiritual upbringing, filled with the obedience of Allāh Most High, and a deep love of the Messenger of Allāh ﷺ. His noble family was famous for its learning, piety, righteousness, generosity and the study of the noble Qur'ān and the noble sciences of the religion. The grandfather of Shaykh Ṣāliḥ, after whom he was named (Shaykh Ṣāliḥ al-Rifā'ī ﷺ) was one of the hardworking scholars of al-Azhar. After emigrating from Egypt to Dongola, he established circles for the memorization of the noble Qur'ān and gatherings for teaching beneficial knowledge in the Grand Mosque [of Dongola]. He would devote his heart and mind, and his entire body to knowledge and the Qur'ān. Shaykh Ṣāliḥ al-Ja'farī inherited from his grandfather the love of knowledge, worship, and turning away from the adornments of the worldly life. At the age of fourteen, Shaykh Ṣāliḥ memorized the Qur'ān with its rules and different recitation styles at the hands of Shaykh 'Alī Abū 'Awf al-Sanhūrī ﷺ and Sayyid Ḥasan Effendī ﷺ, both of whom

3 For a detailed biography of the Shaykh, as according to his family members and students, please see our forthcoming work: The Bountiful Treasure: The Life and Spiritual Methodology of Shaykh Ṣāliḥ al-Ja'farī (2022).

memorized it with his grandfather. Shaykh Ṣāliḥ also studied Mālikī fiqh with Shaykh ʿAlī Muḥammad Jawwī ﵀, one of the scholars of al-Azhar and the Imām of the Grand Mosque of Dongola.

Shaykh Ṣāliḥ's father was Sayyid Muḥammad Ṣāliḥ ﵀, who was known for his hardworking attitude and responsibility towards taking care of both his immediate and extended family. During the night, he would stand in worship of his Lord until the time nearing dawn; after which he would go to the Grand Mosque, open the door, and light the lamps. He would wait until the worshippers would come and then perform the Adhān for the Fajr prayer, and then lead the prayer. After that, he would return home and wake his family up to pray before sunrise. Sayyid Muḥammad Ṣāliḥ was a strong and active man, and he did not like to see people being lazy. His farm was one of the best in Dongola, and he was known in his city as 'The Lion' because of his strength and intensity in work. He performed the Ḥajj ten times and would serve the pilgrims, take care of their needs, and would carry weapons in order to defend against robbers and bandits that would steal goods from the pilgrims on the Ḥajj route. He would travel from Sudan to Egypt to visit his forefathers from the *Ahl al-Bayt* and the resting places of the saints and scholars. He would also visit his son Shaykh Ṣaliḥ in al-Azhar. These pure characteristics show the purity of this noble lineage. Sayyid Muḥammad Ṣāliḥ remained persistent in prayer and worship, consistently performing his prayers in congregation and always making sure that he would be in the first row throughout his life.

**Journey to al-Azhar for Knowledge**

Shaykh Ṣāliḥ al-Jaʿfarī spent his youth studying various sciences of Islamic knowledge until the time came for him to travel to al-Azhar. An indication came from Shaykh ʿAbd al-ʿĀlī b. Sayyid Aḥmad b. Idrīs ﵀, which was the cause for his firm resolve and decision to travel. Shaykh Ṣāliḥ says, "Before I arrived at al-Azhar, one of my townspeople brought the first volume of al-Nawawī's commentary on Ṣaḥīḥ Muslim. I borrowed it from him and began to read it diligently. I saw Shaykh ʿAbd al-ʿĀlī al-Idrīsī ﵀ in a vision, sitting on a chair with provisions for travel around him. I heard someone say "The shaykh wants to travel to al-Azhar in Egypt." I went and greeted him, and kissed his hand. He said to me with all seriousness, "Knowledge is taken from the hearts of men, not from books!" He repeated that and then I woke from my sleep – my Lord had inspired me to travel to al-Azhar." Shaykh Ṣāliḥ was directed towards al-Azhar to study with the scholars in their gatherings, because of the science and the knowledge it contains, which can hardly be found elsewhere – it gathered all the sciences. Shaykh Ṣāliḥ says in one of his books that he saw Shaykh Aḥmad b. Idrīs ﵀ saying to him in a vision,

"Allāh is with you. Study fiqh according to the four schools." Shaykh Ṣāliḥ said, "When I awoke, I told one of my teachers of this vision and he said, 'If this vision is true, then its interpretation is that you should travel to al-Azhar – where fiqh is taught according to the four schools'". Allāh fulfilled this vision! Shaykh Ṣāliḥ continued and said, "And when I reached al-Azhar, I found the ḥadith scholar Shaykh Muḥammad Ibrāhīm al-Samaluti, teaching al-Nawawī's commentary on Sahih Muslim, so I sat down to listen to him, and heard him teaching the ḥadith: "There is no hijra after the Opening of Makka, but only Jiḥad and intention. When you are called upon to go, then go forth!".

When Shaykh Ṣāliḥ reached Egypt, he joined al-Azhar and remained there completely. It was for the sake of seeking knowledge that he left his country and homeland, leaving his family and children, so he would not waste even a moment in something other than gaining knowledge or benefiting from the great scholars of al-Azhar at that time. He completed his studies with sincerity and dedication, and received the Alimiyya certificate, the highest degree from al-Azhar (12 year program), according to its old system. Later, when al-Azhar began to reorganize their education system, and develop specializations and set up different faculties, Shaykh Ṣāliḥ attended the Faculty of Sharīʿa, where he obtained another degree, not out of necessity but from love for knowledge. The diligent student would only leave al-Azhar to visit his grandfather, Imām al-Husayn and the *Ahl al-Bayt*.

**Becoming a teacher and the Imām at al-Azhar**

Shaykh Ṣāliḥ did not restrict himself to only the obligations of his job. Rather, he taught and gave sermons in all corners of al-Azhar. Hearts rushed towards him because of the beneficial knowledge Allāh had bestowed upon him, and his sincere and truthful advice. Students came from both inside and outside al-Azhar, such that some of those working with him at al-Azhar began to complain because of the Shaykh's stepping forward to teach and lecture, envying his acceptance among people. This continued until an opportunity came for the Shaykh to display the breadth of his knowledge and suitability for such a great place – whereby objectors submitted, arguers were silenced, and lovers of the Shaykh made happy. This opportunity arose after the passing of one of his teachers, the erudite scholar Shaykh Yūsuf al-Dijwī (d.1365 AH–1946 CE). The Scholars and students of al-Azhar gathered to bid farewell to their great teacher. Shaykh Dr. Muḥammad Rajab al-Bayūmī, the renowned teacher of literature and rhetoric at al-Azhar, relates the story:

One of the situations in which the magnificence of Shaykh Ṣāliḥ reached a peak was in his eulogy of his great teacher Shaykh Yūsuf al-Dijwī. I was a student in the Faculty of Arabic Language when the shaykh's passing was announced along with the time of his funeral prayer. I rushed quickly to bid the shaykh farewell, and the event was incredibly moving. In front was a group of the great and senior scholars, led by Shaykh Muṣṭafā ʿAbd al-Razzāq ؒ (Shaykh al-Azhar, d.1366 AH-1947 CE). When the procession reached its end at the grave, Shaykh Ṣāliḥ stood to give a speech eulogizing his teacher. He began by drawing on the words of the Messenger of Allāh ﷺ, 'Allāh does not take away knowledge by taking it away from the people, but takes it away by the death of the scholars, until none of them remain, and people will take ignorant leaders, who when consulted, answer without knowledge. So, they will go astray and will lead the people astray.

Then Shaykh Ṣāliḥ began to explain the great rank of the deceased scholar, praising his stance against the innovators and atheists. The magnanimity of the scene, the tremendousness of the occasion, and the gathering of people were things that would make the soul and speech of the eulogizer expand greatly and flow beautifully, pouring forth with emotion and excitement. His voice contained a sadness that moved the souls of those listening and swept their hearts away. The speaker had barely finished his eulogy before the Shaykh of al-Azhar asked about him in amazement and quickly rushed to appoint him as a teacher in al-Azhar. His official appointment gave him a stability that muted those who criticised the advancement of the shaykh because of their own envy, considering him to transgress the bounds of someone in his situation when he began to give daily sermons without tiring. These people were a minority, though, and came to know of their mistake and submitted to the truth after their defiance."[4]

### The Friday Lessons at al-Azhar

Shaykh Ṣāliḥ held a lesson after the Friday prayer in al-Azhar. This lesson was a religious and spiritual school unto itself, with its *ʿilm* taken from the Qurʾān, the Sunna, and the Sharīʿa. And it was infused with the spirituality of Sufism and its spiritual upbringing, so that it revealed the Sufi truths. He poured from himself into his lessons with *īmān* from his soul, so that the purity of asceticism, piety, and righteousness appeared, and the lights of guidance shined, and the purity of the *fiṭra* showed. The shaykh would welcome questions and answer them with patience, love and gentleness. He delivered these answers in a way that was readily received and easy to understand for the listeners, and this, coupled with his mastery of the sciences, attracted masses of people from different facets of society.

---

[4] Majallah al-Azhar, p.1874, Shawwāl 1399 AH – September 1979 CE

## His Passing and Legacy

Shaykh Ṣāliḥ al-Jaʿfarī spent his life in the constant remembrance of Allāh, calling and guiding people to Him and in following the Sunna of the Prophet. He returned to his Lord, well-pleased and well-pleasing, on 18th Jumāda al-Awwal 1399 AH (16th April 1979 CE) and is buried next to his mosque in Darrāsa, Cairo. Shaykh Ṣāliḥ would often come to this very place as a student, to read and memorize various works that he was studying and would refer to it as the 'Garden of the ever-living ones'. Students of al-Azhar flock to his maqam, to memorize the Qurʾān, the books of the Sunna, and primary texts in the religious sciences, because of this blessing of Shaykh Ṣāliḥ. He said, "My path is the Qurʾān, (the seeking and application of beneficial) knowledge and God-consciousness, and praising the Messenger of Allāh, the eraser of all misguidance." The Shaykh has a beautiful legacy of published works and an established spiritual path, which has disciples and students all over the world, from the Middle East, Malaysia, North Africa, India, Nigeria, South Africa, North America and Europe. Many of the senior scholars of al-Azhar today, were students of Shaykh Ṣāliḥ, and they often cite him in their lessons. Some of these scholars include Shaykh Dr. ʿĀlī Jumuʿa (the former Grand Mufti of Egypt), Shaykh Dr. Fatḥī Hijāzī (Senior Professor at the Faculty of Arabic Language at al-Azhar University) and the late Shaykh Dr. Aḥmad Ṭāḥā Rayyān (the Head of the Mālikī Scholars of Egypt, d. 2021 CE). The late son of Shaykh Ṣāliḥ, Shaykh ʿAbd al-Ghanī al-Jaʿfarī, established many masājid across Egypt, which in addition to being centers (sāḥat, lit. courtyards) for the spiritual path of his father (al-Ṭarīqa al-Jaʿfarīyya), offer bakeries, libraries, hospitals, pharmacies, Qurʾān memorization schools and adult learning classes – all of which are free to those unable to pay. These centers, including the principal center in Darrāsa, Cairo, host twice weekly gatherings of Qurʾān recitation, lessons of religious and spiritual knowledge, dhikr, ṣalawāt and praise of the Prophet and the *Ahl al-Bayt* in the form of madīḥ, taken from the 12 volume collection that Shaykh Ṣāliḥ wrote, known as the Dīwān al-Jaʿfarī.

How fitting it is that Shaykh Ṣāliḥ al-Jaʿfarī is buried near his grandfather, Imām al-Ḥusayn and al-Azhar al-Sharīf! May Allāh illuminate his grave and make it a garden from the gardens of Paradise. May he drink from the hand of the one he loved, and enter the highest Paradise, holding his blessed and noble hand, alongside all his family, teachers, disciples, students and those who loved him. Āmīn.

**-1-**

## The Family of My Beloved, You Are My Cure

صَلِّ يَا رَبِّ ثُمَّ سَلِّمْ عَلَى مَنْ
هُوَ لِلخَلْقِ رَحْمَةٌ وَ شِفَاءُ

Send prayers, Lord, then greetings on the one
who to creation is a mercy and healing

آلَ بَيْتِ الحَبِيبِ أَنْتُمْ شِفَاءِي
وَ رِضَاكُمْ هُوَ المُنَى وَ رِضَاءِي

Members of the beloved's household, you are my cure,
and your pleasure is indeed my wish and my pleasure

إِنْ دَخَلْتُ المَقَامَ يَرْتَاحُ قَلْبِي
فَبِهِ رَاحَتِي وَ كُلُّ مُنَاءِي

When I enter the maqam[5], my heart is happy
therein is my rest, and all my desires

5 Burial site.

فَشُهُودُ الرِّحَابِ مِنْكُمْ حَيَاةٌ
كَحَيَاةِ الجِنَانِ لِلسُّعَدَاءِ

Witnessing magnanimity from you is life!
As is the life of Paradise for the blissful

وَ ضِيَاءُ النَّبِيِّ يُضْوِى لِقَوْمٍ
جَالِسُوكُمْ بِعَبْرَةٍ وَ بُكَاءِ

The Prophet's radiance illuminates the people
your sitting companions, with tears and weeping

وَ غَمَامُ الخَيْرَاتِ يُمْطِرُ غَيْثاً
لِمُحِبٍّ يَجِيءُ فِي الظَّلْمَاءِ

Copious rain pours down from the clouds of goodness
for the lover who comes in the darkness

وَ كِتَابُ الإِلَهِ يُتْلَى جِهَاراً
بِمَدِيحٍ لِقَدْرِكُمْ وَ ثَنَاءِ

God's Book is recited openly
as a panegyric of your rank, and an encomium

وَ لَكُمْ رِزْقُكُمْ مِنَ اللّهِ يَأْتِي
كُلَّ حِيْنٍ فِي رَوْضَةٍ غَنَّاءِ

Yours is a provision from Allah that arrives
every moment in a luxuriant orchard

وَ لَبِسْتُمْ مِنَ الثِّيَابِ حَرِيراً
أَخْضَرَ اللَّوْنِ مُفْرِحًا بِبَهَاءِ

You wear garments of silk
green in color, pleasing in its brilliance

وَ شَرِبْتُمْ شَرَابَ قُدْسٍ وَ طُهْرٍ
وَ حُبِيتُمْ بِرَحْمَةٍ وَ جَزَاءِ

You drank a beverage of sacredness and purity
and you were favored by mercy and reward

شَأْنُكُمْ فِي الدُّنَا زَهَادَةُ فَانٍ
طَالَمَا جُدْتُمُ بِدَارِ فَنَاءِ

Your affair in this world is abstinence from that which perishes
how often you strove in an abode of extinction!

وَ سَكَنْتُمْ فَوْقَ الخُيُولِ لِحَرْبٍ
وَ سَكَنْتُمْ فِي الخُلْدِ فِي الشُّهَدَاءِ

You dwelled on horseback engaged in warfare
and in everlastingness among the martyrs, you dwelled

طَالَمَا نَوَّرَ الظَّلَامَ قِيَامٌ
لِعَلِيٍّ وَ سَايِرِ الأَبْنَاءِ

How many times darkness was enlightened by striving
from ʾAlī and the rest of the offspring

هُمْ نُجُومٌ لِمَنْ تَحَيَّرَ فِينَا

وَ نَعِيمٌ لِسَايِرِ الفُقَرَاءِ

They are the stars for those among us bewildered,
a bliss to the rest of the spiritual travellers

وَ ضِيَاءٌ بِاللَّيْلِ مِنْ بَعْدِ شَمْسٍ

وَبُدُوْرٌ تَدُوْرُ فِي الأَنْحَاءِ

A light at night succeeding the sun,
and full moons in all directions rotating

وَ كَمَالٌ مِنَ النَّبِيِّ تَوَالَى

بِجَلَالٍ عَلَيْهِم بِوَلَاءِ

A perfection from the Prophet poured continually
majesty on them through affection

وَ سَلَامٌ عَلَيْهِمُ كُلَّ حِيْنٍ

مَا تَغَنَّى القَمْرِيُّ كَالوَرْقَاءِ

Greetings to them every time
the turtledove sings like the dove

وَ سَلَامٌ عَلَيْهِمُ مِنْ مُحِبٍّ

يَمْلَأُ الكَوْنَ سَايِرَ الأَرْجَاءِ

Salutations to them from a lover,
which fills the cosmos from all sides

وَ صَلاةٌ مَعَ السَّلامِ لِطَهَ
سَيِّدُ الكَوْنِ صَادِقُ الأَنْبَاءِ

May prayers and greetings be upon ṬāHā,
master of the universe, whose reports are truthful

وَ عَلَى الآلِ وَ الصَّحَابَةِ طُرًّا
وَ جَمِيعِ الأَخْيَارِ وَ الأُمَرَاءِ

On his family and on the Companions without exception,
on all the choice ones and the leaders

عَدَّمَا صَالِحٌ تَغَنَّى بِمَدْحٍ
آلَ بَيْتِ الحَبِيبِ أَنْتُمْ شِفَائِي

So long as Ṣāliḥ sings a eulogy
for the members of the beloved's household, you are my healing.

-2-

## Al-Maqbūla, The Accepted Qaṣīda[6]

صَلَّى اللّٰهُ عَلَى مُحَمَّدٍ

صَلَّى اللّٰهُ عَلَيْهِ وَ سَلَّمْ

May Allah send prayers on Muḥammad
May He send him prayers and greetings of peace

رَوْضَةُ الهَادِى نَبِينَا

هُيِّئَتْ لِلمُتَّقِينَا

The Rawḍa[7] of the Guide, our Prophet
has been readied for the people of taqwā,

كُلُّ مَنْ قَالُوا رَضِينَا

بِالحَبِيبْ مَوْلَاىْ مُحَمَّدْ

All those who say, 'We are pleased'
with the Beloved, my master Muḥammad

6 Also known as 'The Rawḍa of the Guide'.
7 Rawḍa is the resting place of the Messenger of Allah ﷺ lit. garden or meadow.

حُبُّهُ عَيْنُ الكَمَالِ

جَاهُهُ عَالٍ وَ غَالِي

Love for him is the source of perfection
his status is lofty and precious

صَحْبُهُ خَيْرُ الرِّجَالِ

بَايَعُوا الهَادِى مُحَمَّدْ

His Companions are the best of people
they pledged allegiance to the guide Muḥammad

وَجْهُهُ فَاقَ البُدُورَا

زَادَهُ المَوْلَى سُرُورَا

His face surpassed the full moon
The Master increases him in happiness

قَدْ بَدَا فِي الكَوْنِ نُورَا

قَبْلَ خَلْقِ اللّٰهْ مُحَمَّدْ

He appeared in the cosmos as light
before all the creation of Allah, was Muḥammad!

حُبُّهُ فَرْضٌ وَ حَتْمُ

مَدْحُهُ خَيْرٌ وَ غُنْمُ

Love of him is mandatory and an obligation
praise for him is goodness and profit

لَيْسَ يَأْتِي القَلْبَ هَمُّ
لِلَّذِي يَهْوِى مُحَمَّدْ

No worry seizes the heart
of one who is in love with Muḥammad

بَحْرُ عِلْمِ اللَّهِ أَحْمَدْ
كُلُّ مَنْ يَلْقَاهُ يَسْعَدْ

The ocean of the knowledge of Allah is Aḥmad
whoever meets him is felicitous

حَوْضُهُ الصَّافِي المُبَرَّدْ
لِلَّذِي يَعْشَقْ مُحَمَّدْ

His pool, the pure and cooled
is for ardent lovers of Muḥammad

يَفْتَحُ اللَّهُ العَوَالِمْ
بِإِمَامٍ لِلمَكَارِمْ

Allah opens the worlds
through the Imām of noble traits

لِجَمِيعِ الرُّسْلِ خَاتِمْ
الحَبِيبْ مَوْلَايْ مُحَمَّدْ

A seal for all the Messengers,
the Beloved, my master Muḥammad

خَيْرُ خَلْقِ اللَّهِ طَهَ

مِثْلُ شَمْسٍ فِي ضُحَاهَا

The best of Allah's creation, ṬāHā,
like the sun in its midmorning brightness

هَذِهِ الدُّنْيَا نَرَاهَا

فِي ضِيَاءٍ مِنْ مُحَمَّدْ

This world we do see
by a light from Muḥammad

أَكْحَلُ العَيْنَيْنِ أَدْعَجْ

نُورُهُ المَحْبُوبُ أَبْلَجْ

His eyes lined by kohl, deep-black
his beloved light, serenely beautiful

أَشْنَبُ الأَسْنَانِ أَفْلَجْ

فَاقَ رُسْلَ اللَّهْ مُحَمَّدْ

With lovely white teeth, well-spaced
surpassing all the messengers of Allah, Muḥammad

وَجْهُهُ يَا نَاسُ نَايِرْ

سَيِّدِي مَوْلَى البَشَايِرْ

His face, O people, is luminous
My liege, the master of glad tidings

ذُخْرُنَا نُورُ البَصَايِرْ

إِسْمُهُ الهَادِى مُحَمَّدْ

Our treasure, the light of insights
his name is the Guide, Muḥammad

قَدْرُهُ العَالِى المُفَضَّلْ

وَصْفُهُ الغَالِى المُكَمَّلْ

His rank lofty, favored,
his qualities perfected and priceless

وَحْىُ رَبِّى قَدْ تَنَزَّلْ

لِلحَبِيبْ مَوْلَاىْ مُحَمَّدْ

The revelation of my Lord would descend
on the Beloved, my master Muḥammad

فَضْلُهُ عَمَّ النَّوَاحِى

لِظَلَامِ الكُفْرِ مَاحِى

His bounty encompasses the horizons
the darkness of disbelief, he effaces

فِى الصَّحَارَى وَ البِطَاحِ

أَشْرَقَتْ أَنْوَارُ مُحَمَّدْ

In the deserts and the valleys
shine the lights of Muḥammad

شَرْعُهُ لِلكَوْنِ يَعْمُرْ

وَ بِهِ الأَيَامُ تَفْخَرْ

His Law fills the cosmos with prosperity
and in it the passing days take their pride

دَمْعُ مَنْ يَهْوَاهُ يَقْطُرْ

مِنْ غَرَامٍ فِي مُحَمَّدْ

The tears of his lovers pour down
ardently with desire for Muḥammad

حُسْنُهُ لِلْبَدْرِ أَخْجَلْ

وَ بِهِ غَيْبٌ تَنَزَّلْ

His beauty puts to shame the full moon
and by it the unseen is revealed

وَ جُمُوعَ الكُفْرِ عَطَّلْ

عَزْمُ مَوْلَانَا مُحَمَّدْ

And all of disbelief is invalidated
by the resolution of our master Muḥammad

البَعِيرْ يَشْكُو المَجَاعَهْ

لِلنَّبِيِّ بَيْنَ الجَمَاعَهْ

The camel complains of starvation
to the Prophet amid his associates

قَالَ يَا مَوْلَى الشَّفَاعَهْ

كُنْ شَفِيعِي يَا مُحَمَّدْ

It said, 'My master, please, intercede!
be my intercessor, O Muḥammad!'

نَادَتْ الهَادِى غَزَالَهْ

تَشْتَكِي تُبْدِى مَقَالَهْ

The gazelle called to the Guide
complaining with clear speech

يَا إِمَاماً لِلرِّسَالَهْ

كُنْ ضَمِينِي يَا مُحَمَّدْ

'O Imām of prophecy
be my guarantor, O Muḥammad'

هَذِهِ الدُّنْيَا كَسَاعَهْ

إِجْعَلِ الأَعْمَالَ طَاعَهْ

This dunya is but a moment,
make actions an obedience to him!

وَ اشْتَرِى خَيْرَ بِضَاعَهْ

زَوْرَةَ الهَادِى مُحَمَّدْ

Purchase the best of commodities,
a visit to the Guide, Muḥammad

هَذِهِ الدُّنْيَا تَزُولُ

وَ البَقَا لَيْسَ يَطُولُ

This dunya is fleeting,
and what remains of it is not long

أَيْنَ مَنْ يَمْشِي يَقُولُ

كُنْ شَفِيعِي يَا مُحَمَّدْ

Where are those who come saying
'Be my intercessor, O Muḥammad'

رَبَّنَا يَسِّرْ وَ سَهِّلْ

زَوْرَةَ المُخْتَارِ عَجِّلْ

Our Lord, facilitate and make easy
our visit to the Chosen one hasten!

دَمْعُنَا يَهْمِي وَ يَنْزِلْ

مِنْ غَرَامٍ فِي مُحَمَّدْ

Our tears stream down in a flow
from ardent love for Muḥammad

رَبَّنَا هَيِّئْ طَرِيقاً

كُنْ لَنَا رَبِّي رَفِيقاً

Our Lord, make ready a path
be for us, my Lord, a companion

كَىْ نَرَى بَدْراً شَفِيقاً

الحَبِيبْ مَوْلَاىْ مُحَمَّدْ

In order the we see the compassionate full moon
the Beloved, my master Muḥammad

ظَنُّنَا فِيكَ جَمِيلُ

أَنْتَ يَا رَبِّي وَكِيلُ

Our expectation of You is beauty
You, O my Lord, are the Guardian

وَ النَّبِيُّ نِعْمَ الكَفِيلُ

الحَبِيبْ مَوْلَاىْ مُحَمَّدْ

And the Prophet, is the best guarantor
the Beloved, my master, Muḥammad

كُلُّنَا يَرْجُو البِشَارَةْ

بِالرَّحِيلْ نَحْوَ الزِّيَارَةْ

All of us hope for glad tidings
of setting out for the visit

حَبَّذَا تِلْكَ التِّجَارَةْ

زَوْرَةُ الهَادِى مُحَمَّدْ

How excellent is that trade
paying visit to the Guide, Muḥammad

أَيْنَ أَصْحَابُ الكَمَالِ

أَيْنَ سَادَاتُ الرِّجَالِ

Where are the owners of perfection?
Where are the masters of men?

أَنْفَقُوا مِنْ خَيْرِ مَالِ

قَاصِدِينْ مَوْلَاىْ مُحَمَّدْ

They spend out of the best wealth
aiming for my master, Muḥammad

دَمْعُهُمْ يَقْطُرْ وَ بَادِى

كُلَّمَا حَلُّوا بِوَادِى

Their tears stream, and the Bedouin
whenever they descend the valley

قَصْدُهُمْ خَيْرُ العِبَادِ

الحَبِيبْ مَوْلَاىْ مُحَمَّدْ

Their goal is the best of servants
the Beloved, my master, Muḥammad

سَارَ بِالرَّحْمٰنِ سَارَا

رَكْبُهُمْ يَطْوِى القِفَارَا

They travel by the Most Merciful
their mounts traverse the desert swiftly

وَ رَأَيْنَاهُمْ جِهَارًا
عَاشِقِينْ مَوْلَاىْ مُحَمَّدْ

We see them clearly
ardent lovers of my master, Muḥammad

حَرُّ هَاتِيكَ البَوَادِى
مِثْلُ ثَلْجٍ مِنْ وِدَادِ

The heat of the desert becomes
like snow, from love

حِصْنُهُمْ خَيْرُ العِبَادِ
رَحْمَةُ الهَادِى مُحَمَّدْ

Their fortress is the choicest of servants,
the Mercy, the Guide, Muḥammad

أُسْكُبِ الدَّمْعَ حَلَالَا
عِنْدَمَا تَلْقَى الهِلَالَا

Pour forth tears, legitimate!
When you meet the crescent

مِنْ بَعِيدٍ قَدْ تَلَالَا
فِيهِ نُورٌ مِنْ مُحَمَّدْ

From afar glittering,
therein a light from Muḥammad

هَذِهِ الخَضْرَاءُ تَظْهَرْ
نُورُهَا لِلعَقْلِ يَبْهَرْ

This green [dome] appears,
its light overwhelms the intellect

عِنْدَ رُؤْيَاهَا تَحَدَّرْ
دَمْعُ مَنْ يَعْشَقْ مُحَمَّدْ

On seeing it, tears
are shed by those loving Muḥammad

رَوْضَةُ الهَادِي نَبِينَا
تُفْرِحُ القَلْبَ الحَزِينَا

The Rawḍa of the Guide, our Prophet
gladdens the heart steeped in sorrow

أَبْشِرُوا يَا زَائِرِينَا
بِالشَّفَاعَهْ مِنْ مُحَمَّدْ

Glad tidings to you, our visitors,
of intercession from Muḥammad

هَذِهِ الرَوْضَةُ أَبْشِرْ
قَدْ وَصَلْنَا لِلمُبَشِّرْ

This Rawḍa, rejoice, as we arrived
to the bringer of glad tidings

أَمْرَ دُنْيَا لَا تُفَكِّرْ
وَ انْظُرِ الهَادِى مُحَمَّدْ

Do not mind the affairs of the dunya,
look instead at the Guide, Muḥammad

كُلُّ مَنْ زَارَ المَقَامَا
فَالنَّبِيُّ رَدَّ السَّلَامَا

Whoever visits the maqam,
the Prophet returns the greetings

يَعْرِفُ الخَلْقَ تَمَامَا
بَشِّرُوا زُوَّارْ مُحَمَّدْ

He recognizes the creation in entirety
give glad tidings to those visiting Muḥammad!

هَامَتِ الأَرْوَاحُ حُبَّا
دَمْعُنَا قَدْ سَالَ صَبَّا

The souls are ecstatic out of love
copiously our tears flow down

نَالَتِ الزُّوَّارُ قُرْبَا
لِلحَبِيبْ مَوْلَاىْ مُحَمَّدْ

The visitors attain nearness
to the Beloved, my master Muḥammad

يَا حَبِيبَ المُتَّقِينَا

وَ سِرَاجاً وَ مُبِينَا

O Beloved of those who have taqwā,
a guiding light and clear proof

يَا أَبَا القَاسِمْ دُعِينَا

فَأَتَيْنَا يَا مُحَمَّدْ

O Abul-Qāsim, we were called,
so we came, O Muḥammad

مَرْحَبَا يَا مُصْطَفَانَا

حُبُّكَ الغَالِي أَتَانَا

Welcome, O Chosen one!
Your precious love came to us

مِنْ بَعِيدٍ قَدْ دَعَانَا

لِلحَبِيبْ مَوْلَایْ مُحَمَّدْ

From afar it called us
to the Beloved, my master Muḥammad

كَيْ نَرَى ذَاكَ المَقَامَا

فِيهِ بَدْرٌ قَدْ تَسَامَى

In order to witness that maqam
in it is a full moon soaring to heights

وَأَخُو الشَّوْقِ تَسَامَى

مِنْ هُيَامٍ فِي مُحَمَّدْ

And the brothers of longing vie with each other
out of ardent love for Muḥammad

يَا شَفِيعًا لِلذُّنُوبِ

وَ غِيَاثاً فِي الكُرُوبِ

O intercessor for sins,
O succour in hardships

وَ ضِيَاءً لِلقُلُوبِ

أَنْتَ نُورٌ يَا مُحَمَّدْ

O illumination for the hearts,
you are light, O Muḥammad

جَاهُكَ المَرْجُو عَظِيمُ

أَنْتَ مِفْضَالٌ كَرِيمُ

Your expected rank is magnificent
you are the pre-eminent, generous,

وَ رَءُوفٌ وَ رَحِيمٌ

وَ عَفُوٌّ يَا مُحَمَّدْ

Compassionate, merciful,
forbearing, O Muḥammad

أَبْشِرُوا يَا مَنْ رَأَيْتُمْ
رَوْضَةَ الهَادِى وَ زُرْتُمْ

Rejoice, O you who see
the Rawḍa of the Guide, and visit

عِنْدَ رَبِّ العَرْشِ كُنْتُمْ
زَائِرِينْ مَوْلَاىْ مُحَمَّدْ

In the sight of the Lord of the Throne you are
visiting my master Muḥammad

قَدَّرَ المَوْلَى السَّعَادَةْ
وَ دَعَاكُمْ لِلعِبَادَةْ

Happiness, the Master decreed
and called you to His worship

هَذِهِ الحُسْنَى زِيَادَةْ
زَوْرَةُ الهَادِى مُحَمَّدْ

This beauty is an increase
visiting the Guide, Muḥammad

سَعْدُكُمْ يَا مَنْ تَزَوْرُوا
وَجْهُكُمْ يَعْلُوهُ نُورُ

Your felicity, O you who visit!
Light will cover your faces

رَبُّكُمْ رَبٌّ غَفُورُ

لِلَّذِى قَدْ زَارَ مُحَمَّدْ

Your Lord is a pardoning Lord
to whomever visits Muḥammad

لَوْ رَأَيْنَا الوَاقِفِينَا

لَوْ رَأَيْنَا القَاعِدِينَا

If only we saw those standing
if only we saw those sitting

لَوْ رَأَيْنَا السَّايِلِينَا

الشَّفَاعَهْ مِنْ مُحَمَّدْ

If only we saw those seeking
intercession from Muḥammad

نُورُ خَيْرِ الخَلْقِ يُجْلَى

وَ كِتَابُ اللّهِ يُتْلَى

The light of the best of creation is manifest
and the Book of Allah is recited

وَ عُلُومُ الشَّرْعِ تُمْلَى

عِنْدَ مَوْلَانَا مُحَمَّدْ

The sciences of the Sharīʾa dictated
at the place of our master Muḥammad

إِنْ رَجَعْتُمْ بِالسَّلَامَهْ
أَخْبِرُوا أَهْلَ المَلَامَهْ

If you return in safety,
apprise the people of blame

كَيْ يَجِيئُوا مِنْ تِهَامَهْ
لِلحَبِيبْ مَوْلَاىْ مُحَمَّدْ

So that they come from Tihāma
to the Beloved, my master Muḥammad

عَرِّفُوهُمْ بِالمَقَامِ
أَخْبِرُوهُمْ بِالهُيَامِ

Acquaint them with the maqam
inform them of the ardent passion

أَيْقِظُوهُمْ مِنْ مَنَامِ
كَيْ يَزُورُوا لِمُحَمَّدْ

Awaken them from their sleep
so that they visit Muḥammad

لَوْ عَلِمْتُمْ يَا عَوَازِلْ
مَا سَكَنْتُمْ فِي المَنَازِلْ

If only you knew, O secluded!
You would not reside in your homes

مَا لَنَا فِي القَلْبِ شَاغِلْ
كُلُّنَا يَهْوَى مُحَمَّدْ

No distraction pervades our heart
all of us are in love with Muḥammad

قَدْ سَرَيْنَا بِالمَطَايَا
لِلنَّبِيِّ خَيْرِ البَرَايَا

We set out on the mounts
to the Prophet, the best of existents,

سَيِّدِي كَنْزِ العَطَايَا
الحَبِيبْ مَوْلَايْ مُحَمَّدْ

My master, the treasure of gifts,
the Beloved, my master Muḥammad

حُبُّهُ يُحْيِي القُلُوبَا
يَغْفِرُ اللَّهُ الذُّنُوبَا

Love for him enlivens the hearts
Allah forgives the sins

يَسْتُرُ اللَّهُ العُيُوبَا
بِالحَبِيبْ مَوْلَايْ مُحَمَّدْ

Allah covers the faults
by the Beloved, my master Muḥammad

يَا رَسُولَ اللّٰهِ نَادِى

أَهْلَ حُبٍّ وَ وِدَادٍ

O Messenger of Allah, the people
of affectionate love did call out

هُمْ بِشَوْقٍ فِى بُعَادٍ

أُدْعُهُمْ مَوْلَاىْ مُحَمَّدْ

With a longing, stirring them from a distance,
invite them, my master Muḥammad

وَ تَوَجَّهْ لِلْمُقَدِّرْ

رَبُّنَا الْمُعْطِى يُيَسِّرْ

And turn to the One Who Decrees
May our Lord, the Giver ease things

بَعْدَ عُسْرٍ كَىْ نُبَدِّرْ

لِلْحَبِيبْ مَوْلَاىْ مُحَمَّدْ

After hardship, that we may hasten
to the Beloved, my master Muḥammad

صَلَاوَاتٌ طَيِّبَاتٌ

زَاكِيَاتٌ نَامِيَاتٌ

Pleasant prayers,
pure, growing,

غَالِيَاتٌ دَاْئِمَاتٌ
لِلحَبِيبْ مَوْلَاىْ مُحَمَّدْ

Precious, perpetual,
to the Beloved, my master Muḥammad

وَ سَلَامُ اللَّهِ يَتْرَى
عَطَّرَ الكَوْنَ وَ مَرَّا

And the peace of Allah quenches
and it fragrances the universe throughout

شَرَحَ الصَّدْرَ وَ سَرَّا
لِلحَبِيبْ مَوْلَاىْ مُحَمَّدْ

Expanding the hearts and gladdening them
for the Beloved, my master Muḥammad

وَ عَلَى الصَّحْبِ الأَفَاضِلْ
كُلِّ مِفْضَالٍ وَ عَامِلْ

And on his companions, the most virtuous
each are pre-eminent and whose actions

بِكِتَابِ اللَّهِ قَائِلْ
وَ كَذَا آلُ مُحَمَّدْ

And speech are in accord with the Book of Allah
likewise the family of Muḥammad

عُمَّ بِالرِّضْوَانِ رَبِّي
خَيْرَ صِدِّيقٍ وَ صَحْبِ

My Lord encompasses with His good pleasure
the best of the truthful and companions [8]

وَ كَذَا الفَارُوقَ حِبِّي
سَكَنَا قُرْبَ مُحَمَّدْ

And the Fārūq[9] as well, my beloved
who resides[10] close to Muḥammad

عُمَّ ذَا النُّورَيْنِ رَبِّي
وَ أَبَا السِّبْطَيْنِ حِبِّي

Envelop Dhun-Nūrayn[11], my Lord,
and the father of the two scions[12], my beloved;

ثُمَّ لِلعَمَّيْنِ رَبِّي
ثُمَّ صَحْباً لِمُحَمَّدْ

Then the two uncles[13], my Lord,
and the Companions of Muḥammad

8 Meaning Sayyidunā Abū Bakr ﷺ
9 Sayyidunā 'Umar ﷺ
10 They are buried with the Prophet ﷺ
11 Sayyidunā 'Uthmān ﷺ
12 The reference is of course to Sayyidunā 'Alī ﷺ father of al-Ḥasan ﷺ and al-Ḥusayn ﷺ
13 Al-'Abbās and Ḥamza ﷺ

$$\text{عُمَّ لِلسِّبْطَيْنِ رَبِّي}$$

$$\text{آلَ خَيْرِ الْخَلْقِ طِبِّي}$$

Envelop the two scions[14], my Lord,
family of the best of creation, my medicine

$$\text{وَ كَذَا الزَّهَرَاءُ تُنْبِي}$$

$$\text{عَنْ كَمَالٍ فِي مُحَمَّدْ}$$

Likewise al-Zahrā'[15] manifest
from the perfections of Muḥammad

$$\text{عُمَّ سُهَّارَ اللَّيَالِي}$$

$$\text{كُلَّ مَنْ لِلْوِرْدِ تَالِي}$$

Encompassing those who stay awake at night
and everyone who recites the *wird*[16]

$$\text{هُمْ رِجَالُ الْإِتِّصَالِ}$$

$$\text{بِالْحَبِيبْ مَوْلَائْ مُحَمَّدْ}$$

They are the men of connection
to the Beloved, my master Muḥammad

---

14 Al-Ḥasan and al-Ḥusayn
15 Al-Zahrā': Sayyida Fāṭima
16 The regular daily portion of structured formulas of remembrance.

عُمَّ سُكَّانَ البَرَارِى
وَ الصَّحَارَى وَ القِفَارِ

Encompassing those who reside in the country
the deserts and wastelands

كُلَّ مَجْذُوبٌ وَ قَارِى
لِلصَّلَاةْ عَلَى مُحَمَّدْ

Every *majdhūb*[17] and reciter
of prayers upon Muḥammad

عُمَّ رَبِّي النَّاسِكِينَا
وَ العِبَادَ الصَّالِحِينَا

Extend, my Lord, upon the devotees
and righteous servants,

وَ الرِّجَالَ الوَاقِفِينَا
عِنْدَ مَوْلَانَا مُحَمَّدْ

And the men standing
before our master Muḥammad

وَ بِهِمْ يَا رَبِّ نَصْرَا
دَائِماً دُنْيَا وَ أُخْرَى

By them, O Lord, give victory
perpetually in this life and the next

17 A follower of the Sufi path who has been pulled by Allah towards the Divine Presence, rather than ascending to it through spiritual wayfaring (sulūk).

أَعْظِمَنْ يَا رَبِّ أَجْرَا
بِالحَبِيبْ مَوْلَایْ مُحَمَّدْ

Magnify, my Lord, a reward
through the Beloved, my master Muḥammad

رَبِّ رُدَّ الحَاسِدِينَا
عَنْ أَذَانَا خَائِبِينَا

My Lord, repel the enviers
from harming us, leaving them disappointed

كُنْ لَنَا عَوْناً مُعِينَا
بِالحَبِيبْ مَوْلَایْ مُحَمَّدْ

Be for us aid and support
by means of the Beloved, my master, Muḥammad

رَبِّ لَا تَجْعَلْ عِدَانَا
تَتَمَكَّنْ مِنْ أَذَانَا

My Lord, do not allow our enemies
to have power to harm us

أُكْسُهُمْ ثَوْباً هَوَانَا
وَ أَجِبْنَا بِمُحَمَّدْ

Clothe them in the robe of disgrace,
answer us [O Lord] by means of Muḥammad

عَجِّلِ الخَوْفَ إِلَيْهِمْ

وَ كَذَا البَأْسَ عَلَيْهِمْ

Hasten fear in them,
and likewise calamity upon them

وَ كَذَا الشَّرَّ لَدَيْهِمْ

وَ انْصُرَنْ آلَ مُحَمَّدْ

And likewise their own evil
and protect the family of Muḥammad

نَاظِمُ الدُّرِّ المُحَرَّرْ

صَالِحٌ مِنْ آلِ جَعْفَرْ

The composer of these scribed pearls
Ṣāliḥ from the tribe of Jaʿfar[18]

يَرْجُو فَضْلاً مِنْكَ أَكْبَرْ

بِالحَبِيبْ مَوْلَاىْ مُحَمَّدْ

From You he hopes for a greater favor
by means of the Beloved, my master Muḥammad

يَرْجُو فَضْلاً لَنْ يَزُولَا

وَ رِضَاءً وَ قَبُولَا

He seeks a bounty that will never end,
and pleasure and acceptance,

18 The shaykh traces his lineage to the Prophet ﷺ through Jaʿfar al-Ṣādiq ؓ

وَ اتِّصَالاً وَ وُصُولَا
بِالحَبِيبْ مَوْلَاىْ مُحَمَّدْ

And connection and arrival
to the Beloved, my master Muḥammad

يَرْجُو فَضْلاً مِنْكَ رَبِّي
زَوْرَةَ المُخْتَارِ حِبِّي

He seeks a bounty from You, my Lord,
the visit to the Chosen one, my Beloved

كُلَّ عَامٍ بَيْنَ صَحْبِ
زَائِرِينْ مَوْلَاىْ مُحَمَّدْ

Every year, among companions
visiting my master, Muḥammad

وَ بِخَيْرٍ فِي الخِتَامِ
نَبْتَغِي نَيْلَ المَرَامِ

And a good end to life,
seeking to gain the goal

بِجِوَارٍ لِلمَقَامِ
فِي بَقِيعٍ يَا مُحَمَّدْ

By proximity to the maqam
in Baqī`[19], O Muḥammad

---

19 Baqī`: a spacious place between a variety of trees. It is also the name of the cemetery of Madīnans.

-3-

## O Family of Aḥmad

يَا آلَ أَحْمَدَ لَا يَزَالُ ضِيَاؤُكُمْ

يُضْوِي قُلُوبَ الوَافِدِينَ إِلَيْكُمُ

O family of Aḥmad, your light remains
illuminating the hearts of the delegations that come to you

المُسْلِمُونَ جَمِيعُهُمْ صَلَّوْا عَلَى

خَيْرِ الأَنَامِ مُحَمَّدٍ وَ عَلَيْكُمُ

The Muslims send prayers, all of them,
on the best of mankind, Muḥammad, and on you

سَارُوا إِلَى خَيْرِ الأَنَامِ بِزَوْرَةٍ

وَ إِلَيْكُمُ جَاءُوا وَ صَلَّوْا وَ سَلَّمُوا

They journey to the best of mankind for a visit
and to you; they come, sending prayers and greetings

وَ المُؤْمِنُونَ يَرَوْنَكُمْ أَبْنَاءَهُ
شَمْساً تُضِيءُ مِنَ السَّمَاءِ إِلَيْهِمُ

The believers see you, his sons,
as a sun casting on them light from the sky

مَنْ مِثْلُكُمْ يَا آلَ أَحْمَدَ فِي الوَرَى
سُدْتُمْ بِفِعْلِ جَمِيلِكُمْ وَ صَبَرْتُمُ

Who is the like of you, O family of Aḥmad, in creation
you lead by your lovely action and are patient

وَ شَهَادَةَ الشُّهَدَاءِ مِنْ فَضْلِ العَلِي
يَا سَادَتِي لِحَيَاتِكُمْ قَدْ نِلْتُمُ

The martyrs' martyrdom a favor from the Exalted
O my masters, in your life you have been successful

إِنْ كَانَ مَسْكَنُ جِسْمِكُمْ فِي رَوْضَةٍ
فَنَرَاكُمُ كُلَّ القُلُوبِ سَكَنْتُمُ

If lodged in a garden is your body,
we see you housed in all the hearts

حَاشَا أُضَامُ وَ فِي الفُؤَادِ وِدَادُكُمْ
وَ مُحِبُّكُمْ يَا سَادَتِي أَكْرَمْتُمُ

Far be it that I am harmed while your love is in my heart
the one who loves you, my masters, you honor

مَنْ مِثْلُكُمْ تَحْتَ العَبَاءِ مُشَرَّفاً
أَكْرِمْ بِكُمْ يَا سَادَتِي شُرِّفْتُمُ

Who are the like of you under the cloak, ennobled
he honored you, my masters, you were ennobled!

فَبِجَدِّكُمْ هَذَا النَّبِيِّ وَ جَاهِهِ
فِي حُبِّكُمْ يَا سَادَتِي لَا نُهْضَمُ

By your Grandfather, this Prophet, and his rank
in loving you, my masters, we are not harmed

وَ بِجَاهِكُمْ عِنْدَ الإِلَهِ وَ فَضْلِكُمْ
أَعْدَاؤُنَا ذَاتَ الشِّمَالِ تَحَطَّمُوا

By your rank with the Divine, and your virtue,
our foes by the sides were shattered

يَا أُسْدَ غَابٍ لَا يَضِيعُ نَزِيلُكُمْ
آجَامُكُمْ تَحْمِي وَ أَنْتُمْ أَنْتُمُ

O forest lions, your guest does not come to ruin
your thickets safeguard, and you, you are:

آلُ النَّبِيِّ وَ آلُ أَفْضَلِ مُرْسَلٍ
عِزُّ مَكَارِمُكُمْ لِقَومٍ أَسْلَمُوا

The family of the Prophet, family of the best of Messengers
honor and your virtues are for a people who submit

إِنْ غَابَ بَدْرُ اللَّيْلِ أَنْتُمْ بَدْرُهُ
أَوْ غَابَتِ الشَّمْسُ المُضِيئَةُ كُنْتُمُ

If the night moon vanishes, you are its full moon
if the illumining sun withdraws, you are:

شَمْساً تُضِيءُ لَدَى القُلُوبِ وَ سِرُّهَا
يَشْفِي قُلُوباً قَدْ أَتَتْ تَتَرَحَّمُ

A sun shining in the hearts, and their secret
heals the hearts that come in search of mercy

أُسْدٌ لَدَى الهَيْجَاءِ إِنْ نَقْعٌ عَلَا
وَ سُيُوفُكُمْ نَجْمٌ يُضِيءُ وَ يَرْجُمُ

Lions in combat, when dust is raised
their swords like a star, illuminating and damning

وَ زَئِيرُكُمْ بَيْنَ الصُّفُوفِ كَأَنَّمَا
رَعْدٌ بِلَيْلٍ بَلْ عَلِيٌّ ضَيْغَمُ

Your roar in the battle lines as if
a night thunder, nay, ʿAlī a lion of broad jawbone

وَ عُلُومُكُمْ بَحْرٌ تَنَاثَرَ دُرُّهُ
حُلْوٌ بِهِ أَسْفَارُ عِلْمٍ يُفْهَمُ

Your sciences, a sea of scattered pearls,
sweet, filled with scrolls of knowledge retained

فَجِهَادُكُمْ بَابٌ لِمَنْ هُوَ دَاخِلٌ
وَ حَدِيثُكُمْ عِلْمٌ لِمَنْ هُوَ يَعْلَمُ

Your Jihād[20] is a gate for anyone who enters
and your speech a science for anyone who learns

فَبِقَتْلِكُمْ فِي اللّهِ كُنْتُمْ قُدْوَةً
لِلرَّاغِبِينَ فَبِالدِّمَاءِ تَوَسَّمُوا

In your killing for the sake of Allah you were a model
for the eager ones, so by blood they were marked

وَ سَكَنْتُمُ دَارَ اللِّقَاءِ وَ طَالَما
حَنَّتْ لَهَا أَرْوَاحُكُمْ وَ حَنَنْتُمُ

You dwelled in the abode of the Encounter, and how often
did your souls move to it, yearning

عَمَّرْتُمُ الأَوْقَاتِ ذِكْراً مُخْلِصاً
وَ بِرَبِّكُمْ حُسْنَ الجَزَاءِ ظَنَنْتُمُ

You filled time with sincere remembrance
expecting from your Lord a good reward

فَجَزَاكُمُ الرَّبُّ الجَلِيلُ كَفِعْلِكُمْ
وَ جِوَارَ جَدِّكُمُ النَّبِيِّ سَكَنْتُمُ

May the Majestic Lord requite you accordingly
with proximity to your Grandfather, the Prophet, you dwell

20 Signifies both spiritual and military struggle.

الخُلْدُ دَارُكُمْ بِظِلٍّ بَارِدٍ
وَ اللَّهُ مِنْ طِيبِ الشَّرَابِ سَقَاكُمُ

Everlastingness is your abode, beneath a cool shade
Allah gives you to drink a pleasant nectar

اللَّهُ فَضَّلَكُمْ وَ أَعْلَى قَدْرَكُمْ
وَ إِلَى الشَّهَادَةِ وَ العُلَا نَادَاكُمُ

Allah favors you and elevates your worth
summoning you to martyrdom and loftiness

سُدْتُمْ بِسَابِقَةٍ وَ فِعْلٍ طَيِّبٍ
وَ الجَدُّ طَابَ وَ أُمُّكُمْ وَ أَبُوكُمُ

By a foreordained lot you ruled, and by a deed agreeable,
pleasant is the Grandfather, your mother and your father

حَسَنٌ هُوَ الشَّمْسُ الَّتِي قَدْ أَشْرَقَتْ
وَ حُسَيْنٌ البَدْرُ الَّذِي بِسَمَاكُمُ

Ḥasan, he is the sun that shines
and Ḥusayn, the full moon in your sky

سَادُوا شَبَابَ الخُلْدِ فِي دَرَجَاتِهِمْ
مَنْ مِثْلُهُمْ فِي الخُلْدِ مَنْ سَاوَاهُمُ

At the head of the youth of eternity in their ranks
who is like them in eternity, who are their equal!

وَ لِزَيْنَبِ بِنْتِ الإِمَامِ مُكَارِمٌ
وَ لِفَاطِمٍ وَ سَكِينَةٍ كُبْرَاهُمُ

For Zaynab, the Imām's daughter, are noble traits
likewise Fātima and Sakina, their eldest

نَبَوِيَّةٍ وَ نَفِيسَةٍ وَ لِزَيْنِهِمْ
وَ لِأَنْوَرٍ وَ لِجَعْفَرٍ مُوسَاهُمُ

Nabawiyya, Nafīsa and their Zayn,
Anwar and Jaʿfar, their Mūsā

وَ لِبَاقِرٍ بَقَرَ العُلُومَ وَ زَيْدِهِمْ
وَ أَفَاضِلٍ سَكَنُوا البَقِيعَ تَرَاهُمُ

Bāqir, who split knowledge open, and their Zayd,
virtuous ones dwelling in al-Baqīʾ you see them

وَ لِحَمْزَةٍ عَبَّاسِهِمْ وَ عَقِيلِهِمْ
طَيَّارِهِمْ طَارُوا إِلَى عَلْيَاهُمُ

Hamza, their ʾAbbās, their ʾAqīl,
their Tayyār[21]; to their heights they flew[22]

21 Jaʿfar b. Abī Ṭālib ﷺ known as Jaʿfar aṭ-Ṭayyār.
22 There is an intended pun here between Ṭayyār and the verb "flew" (ṭārū).

زَهْرَاءُ سَادَتْ وَ ابْنُ عَمِّ المُصْطَفَى
تِلْكَ الأُصُولُ وَ هَذِهِ ذِكْرَاهُمُ

Zahrā' was master, and the cousin of the chosen[23]
those are the roots, and this is their commemoration

فَجِوَارُكُمْ نِعْمَ الجِوَارُ لِمَنْ أَتَى
فِي حَيِّكُمْ يَا سَادَتِي وَ حِمَاكُمُ

How wonderful is their proximity for one who comes
by your lives, my masters, and your protection!

إِنِّي نَزِيلُ الجَاهِ أَرْجُو عَطْفَكُمْ
وَ وِدَادَكُمْ يَا سَادَتِي وَ رِضَاكُمُ

Indeed I am a guest of honor, I hope for your affection
and your love, my masters, and your satisfaction

فَبِنُورِكُمْ يُحْمَى الضَّعِيفُ مِنَ الأَذَى
وَ تُرَدُّ أَعْدَائِي بِسَيْفِ أَبِيكُمُ

By your light, the weak are shielded from harm
and my foes are repelled by the sword of your father

يَا مَنْ هُمُ أَمْنٌ لِمَنْ هُوَ خَائِفٌ
حَاشَا أُضَامُ بِحُبِّهِمْ حَاشَاهُمُ

O those who are security for the fearful person:
far be it that I am harmed by my love for them, far from them!

23 Sayyiduna 'Alī ﷺ

نَادِيكُمُ نَادَى لِكُلِّ مُقَرَّبٍ
أَهْلاً وَ سَهْلاً جَنَّةٌ نَادِيكُمُ

Your caller summoned all those brought near
Welcome! The Garden is your assembly

وَ رَدَدْتُمْ أَهْلَ السَّلَامَ سَلَامَ مَنْ
أَهْدَى السَّلَامَ إِلَيْكُمُ حَيَّاكُمُ

You replied to the people of peace, the greeting
of one who gifts you greeting, saluting you

أَحْيَاكُمُ الرَّبُّ الكَرِيمُ تَفَضُّلاً
شُهَدَاءَ حَقٍّ فِي الهَنَا أَحْيَاكُمُ

The Generous Lord enlivened you bounteously
as martyrs of truth. In bliss He gives you life

وَ ثِيَابُكُمْ مِنْ كُلِّ أَخْضَرَ سُنْدُسٍ
سُبْحَانَ مَنْ أَحْيَاكُمُ وَ كَسَاكُمُ

Your dress is made of every green brocade of silk
glory to the One Who gave you life and enrobed you

وَ طَعَامُكُمْ مَا تَشْتَهِيهِ نُفُوسُكُمْ
وَ اللّٰهُ مِنْ عَيْنِ النَّعِيمِ سَقَاكُمُ

Your food is what satisfies you
and Allah gives you drink from the source of bliss

وَ أَرَاكُمُ النُّورَ البَهِيَّ بِحَضْرَةٍ
وَ لِنُورِهِ العَالِي العَظِيمِ هَدَاكُمُ

I see you as radiant light in the Presence
and to His Majestic Exalted Light He guides you

طُوبَى لِعَبْدٍ قَدْ يَزُورُ ضَرِيحَكُمْ
فَرِحَ الفُؤَادُ لِأَنَّهُ يَلْقَاكُمُ

Blessed is the slave who visits your grave
the heart rejoices as it meets you

وَ الرُّوحُ تَعْرِفُ مَنْ يَزُورُ لِأَنَّهَا
تَدْرِي وَ أَنَّ الرُّوحَ لَا تَقْلَاكُمُ

The soul recognizes those who visit, since it
knows, and the soul does not loathe you

رُفِعَ الحِجَابُ لِمَنْ تَرَفَّعَ قَدْرُهُمْ
وَ هُنَاكَ مَنْ يَحْكِي لَنَا وَ رَآكُمُ

The veil is lifted for the high-ranking people
and there are those who report to us and see you

يَا مُنْكِرِينَ تَنَكَّرُوا وَ تَكَدَّرُوا
الكُلُّ يَعْرِفُ نُكْرَكُمْ وَ أَذَاكُمُ

O deniers ungracious in your turbid hostility
they all know your denial and your harmfulness

إِنْ كَانَ عِنْدَكُمُ المَوَدَّةُ بِدْعَةً
فَمِنَ العَجِيبِ فَبِدْعَةٌ رُؤْيَاكُمُ

If according to you love is innovation,
how remarkable then; your opinion is the innovation!

إِنَّ المَوَدَّةَ مِنْ قَدِيمٍ قَدْ بَدَتْ
وَ النُّكْرُ مِنْكُمْ بِدْعَةٌ وَ قِلَاكُمُ

Indeed, love has emerged from pre-eternity,
and denial and hatred from you is the innovation

عَنْ آلِ أَحْمَدَ تَمْنَعُونَ أَحِبَّةً
عَرَفُوا النَّبِيَّ وَ آلَهُ إِيَّاهُمُ

You prevent lovers from the family of Aḥmad
but the Prophet and his family recognize them

فَأَتَوْهُمُ مِنْ فَرْطِ حُبٍّ فِي الضُّحَى
مُتَشَوِّقِينَ وَ حُبُّهُمْ نَادَاهُمُ

They come out of fervent love in the morning,
longingly, and their love summons them

وَ قُلُوبُهُمْ مَمْلُوءَةٌ بِوِدَادِهِمْ
هَجَرُوا الدِّيَارَ وَ فَارَقُوا سُكْنَاهُمُ

Their hearts are filled with love of them,
they abandon their homes and part with their dwellings

ثُمَّ الصَّلَاةُ عَلَى النَّبِيِّ مُحَمَّدٍ
خَيْرِ الأَنَامِ وَ آلِهِ وَ نُسَلِّمُ

Then blessings on the Prophet Muḥammad,
the best of mankind, and on his family, our greetings

وَ الصَّحْبِ وَ الأَبْرَارِ ثُمَّ أَيِمَّةٍ
قَامُوا بِنَصْرِ الدِّينِ فِيهِ تَقَدَّمُوا

And the companions, the pious, then the Imāms
who aid the Dīn and in it advanced

مَا الجَعْفَرِى يَشْدُو بِمَدْحِ أَحِبَّةٍ
عَلِمُوا المَعَارِفَ وَ العُلُومَ وَ عَلَّمُوا

So long as al-Jaʿfarī chants the praises of lovers
who know and teach knowledge and sciences

سَلِّمْ إِلَهِى إِخْوَتِى وَ أَحِبَّتِى
وَ قَرَابَتِى يَا رَبِّ كُلٌّ يَسْلَمُ

Preserve, my God, my brothers and my beloveds,
and my relatives, O Lord, each one in safety.

-4-

## Seeker of Good

صَلَاةٌ سَلَامٌ عَلَى المُصْطَفَى

نَبِيْنَا مُحَمَّدْ عَلَيْهِ السَّلَامْ

Blessings and peace on the Chosen one
our Prophet Muḥammad, peace be upon him

أَيَا طَالِبَ الخَيْرِ عَرِّجْ عَلَى

دِيَارٍ بِهَا فَاحَ مِسْكُ الخِتَامْ

O seeker of good, halt by
houses, in them diffuses the musk of the seal[24]

إِلَى رَوْضَةٍ فَازَ مَنْ زَارَهَا

لَدَى طَيْبَةٍ عِنْدَ ذَاكَ المَقَامْ

to the Rawḍa whose visitor reaps victory
at a pleasant spot[25] by that maqam

24 The Prophet ﷺ
25 Ṭayba, al-Madīna.

تَرَى بَدْرَهَا فَاقَ بَدْرَ السَّمَا
أَضَاءَ قُلُوبَ الوَرَى بِالتَّمَامْ

You see its full moon surpassing the one in the sky
it fills the hearts of creation completely

تَرَى حُبَّهُ فِي قُلُوبِ الوَرَى
يَزِيدُ وَ يَبْقَى لَدَى كُلِّ عَامْ

You see love for him in the hearts of creation
year by year increasing and enduring

وَ مَنْ زَارَهُ كَانَ فِي رَوْضَةٍ
يَرَى البَدْرَ فِيهَا وَ رَدَّ السَّلَامْ

Whoever visits him at the Rawḍa
he sees in it the full moon, and he returns the greetings

أَيَا رَحْمَةَ اللَّهِ يَا مُصْطَفَى
شَفِيعَ الخَلَائِقِ يَوْمَ الزِّحَامْ

O mercy of Allah, O Chosen one
O intercessor of creatures on the day of jostling

بِجَاهِكَ نَنْجُو وَ نَلْقَى الرِّضَا
وَ نَسْعَى إِلَى البَيْتِ عِنْدَ المَقَامْ

By your rank we are rescued and meet with pleasure
and we hasten to the house by the maqam

وَ نُحْرِمُ فِي مَعْشَرٍ أَسْرَعُوا
وَ لَبَّوْا وَ قَالُوا بِتِلْكَ الخِيَامْ

The *iḥram* we don amid a hurrying crowd
chanting *Labbayk* and speaking in those tents

وَ شَمُّوا لِطِيبِكَ فِي رَوْضَةٍ
وَ كَمْ مِنْ شَجِيٍّ مُحِبٍّ وَ هَامْ

They smell your perfume at the Rawḍa
how many an anxious, infatuated lover!

وَ فَاضَتْ دُمُوعٌ لَدَى رَوْضَةٍ
بِهَا النُورُ يُضْوِى يُزِيلُ الظَّلَامْ

Tears flowing at the Rawḍa
where light illuminates, dispelling darkness

حَبِيبِي طَبِيبِي أَيَا سَيِّدِى
رَجَائِي أَرَاكَ وَ لَوْ فِي المَنَامْ

My beloved, my healer, O my master
my hope is that I see you, even if only in a dream

صَلَاةٌ سَلَامٌ عَلَى المُصْطَفَى
نَبِينَا مُحَمَّدْ عَلَيْهِ السَّلَامْ

Blessings and peace on the Chosen one
our Prophet Muḥammad, peace be upon him

وَ مَا الجَعْفَرِى قَالَ يَرْجُو الرِّضَا
صَلَاةٌ سَلَامٌ يَا خَيْرَ الأَنَامْ

So long as al-Jaʿfarī says, hoping for pleasure,
'prayers and peace to you, best of mankind!'

-5-

## O My Masters!

وَ صَلَاةُ رَبِّي دَايِماً

تَغْشَى النَّبِيَّ حَبِيبَكُمْ

May the blessings of my Lord always
envelop the Prophet, Your Beloved

يَا سَادَتِي لَا تَبْعُدُوا

عَنِّي فَإِنِّي إِبْنُكُمْ

My masters, don't distance yourselves
from me, for I am your son

أَرْجُو الرِّضَا يَا سَادَتِي

مِنْ فَضْلِ رَبِّي عِنْدَكُمْ

I hope for contentment, my masters
from the bounty of my Lord to you

يَا أَهْلَ وُدِّي إِنَّنِي

فِي مِصْرِكُمْ بِجِوَارِكُمْ

O recipients of my affection, verily I am
in your city, in your vicinity

نِعْمَ الْجِوَارُ جِوَارُكُمْ

فِي دَارِ خُلْدٍ إِنَّكُمْ

What a wonderful vicinity is your vicinity!
Indeed you are in the abode of eternity

جَنَّاتُ عَدْنٍ زُخْرِفَتْ

مِنْ أَجْلِكُمْ لِخُلُودِكُمْ

Gardens of Eden embellished
for your sake everlastingly

أَهْلُ الْمَوَدَّةِ أَنْتُمُ

جِبْرِيلُ جَاءَ لِجَدِّكُمْ

You are the people of love
Jibrīl came to your Grandfather

اللّٰهُ شَرَّفَ بَيْتَكُمْ

فِي الذِّكْرِ يُتْلَى طُهْرُكُمْ

Allah ennobled your household
in commemoration, your purity is recited

يَا شَمْسُ يُضْوِى نُورُهَا
تَعْلُو المَنَازِلَ شَمْسُكُمْ

O sun whose light illuminates,
your sun towers over the way-stations

حَاشَا أَضِيعُ وَ إِنَّنِي
مَحْسُوبُكُمْ فِي دَارِكُمْ

Far be it that I am ruined while I
am your protégé in your residence

حَاشَا أُضَامُ وَ إِنَّنِي
مَحْسُوبُكُمْ فِي جَاهِكُمْ

Far be it that I am harmed while I
am your protégé under your glory

حَاشَا أُضَامُ وَ إِنَّنِي
شَاهَدْتُ حُسْنَ كَمَالِكُمْ

Far be it that I am harmed while I
witness your fine perfection

مَنْ زَارَكُمْ نَالَ المُنَى
حَاشَا يُضَامُ نَزِيلُكُمْ

Whoever visits you attains his desire
far be it that your guest is harmed

يَا أَهْلَ وُدِّى أَنْتُمُ

أَهْلُ الرِّضَا لِمُحِبِّكُمْ

O recipients of my affection, you are
the people of satisfaction for your lover!

أَحيَا سَعِيداً سَادَتِي

يُجْلَى الظَّلَامُ بِنُورِكُمْ

I live happily, my masters,
darkness is dispelled by your light

إِنْ كُنْتُ عَبْداً مُذْنِباً

فَالعَفْوُ كَانَ لِجَدِّكُمْ

If I am a sinful slave,
pardon is your Grandfather's trait

وَ بِهِ أَنَالُ مَقَاصِدِى

دُنْيَا وَ أُخْرَى عِنْدَكُمْ

By him I fulfil my aims
in this world and the next in your presence

وَ أَشُمُّ فِي الدُّنْيَا عَلَى

عَهْدٍ طَوِيلٍ طِيْبَكُمْ

I smell in this world, based on
a long covenant, your fragrance

يَا طَيْبَةٌ طَابَتْ بِمَنْ
فَضَلَ الخَلَايِقَ جَدُّكُمْ

O Ṭāyba[26] made pleasant by him
who excelled all creatures, your Grandfather

أَحْيَا سَعِيداً إِنَّنِي
مِنْ فَضْلِ رَبِّي نَسْلُكُمْ

I live happily, I
by the bounty of my Lord, I am your offspring

أَهْلَ العَبَاءِ أَحِبَّتِي
مَا كُنْتُ أَهْوَى غَيْرَكُمْ

People of the cloak, my beloved
Only you I love passionately

نَصَرَ النَّبِيَّ مُحَمَّداً
فِي كُلِّ غَزْوٍ سَيْفُكُمْ

The Prophet Muḥammad was helped
in every battle by your sword

يَلْقَى المَهَانَةَ كُلُّ مَنْ
شَهَرَ العَدَاوَةَ ضِدَّكُمْ

Abasement is the fate of whoever
declares enmity against you

26 Al-Madīna.

اللّٰهُ أَعْلَى قَدْرَكُمْ
اللّٰهُ أَعْظَمَ أَجْرَكُمْ

Allah elevates your status
Allah magnifies your reward

دَارُ الخُلُودِ دِيَارُكُمْ
خَيْرُ الطَّعَامِ طَعَامُكُمْ

Yours is the Abode of Everlastingness
yours is the best of foods

عَيْنُ النَّعِيمِ تَهَيَّأَتْ
طُهْرُ الشَّرَابِ شَرَابُكُمْ

Readied is the spring of blissfulness
yours is the beverage pure

يَا مُطْعِمِينَ طَعَامَكُمْ
لِلسَّائِلِينَ بِدَارِكُمْ

O those offering your food
to beggars at your dwelling

يَا مُكْرَمِينَ بِجَنَّةٍ
خُضْرُ الثِّيَابِ لِبَاسُكُمْ

O those by a Garden honored,
green robes are your attire

يَا مَرْحَباً يَا مَرْحَباً

خَيْرُ الجَزَاءِ جَزَاؤُكُمْ

Welcome, yes, welcome!
Yours is the greatest requital

فِيهَا نَعِيمٌ دَايِمٌ

دُمْتُمْ وَ دَامَ نَعِيمُكُمْ

Therein is a bliss enduring
you are permanent, and permanent is your felicity

يَا مَرْحَباً يَا سَادَتِي

مَلَأَ الوُجُودَ ضِيَاؤُكُمْ

Welcome, my masters!
Filled with your light is existence

بِالمُصْطَفَى لَا تَتْرُكُوا

هَذَا النَّزِيلَ بِبَابِكُمْ

By the Chosen one, do not leave
this guest at your door

يَرْجُوكُمْ فَضْلَ الرِّضَا

مِنْ فَضْلِ رَبِّي رَبِّكُمْ

Hoping for the favor of your pleasure
from the bounty of my Lord, your Lord

أَرْجُو مِنَ اللّٰهِ الَّذِى

أَرْضَاكُمُ فِي عَدْنِكُمْ

I hope from Allah Who
pleased you in His Eden

غُفْرَانَ ذَنْبِي إِنَّنِي

فِي عَطْفِكُمْ بِجِوَارِكُمْ

Pardon from my sins, I
am under your compassion, near you

يَا آلَ بَيْتِ مُحَمَّدٍ

السَّعْدُ فِي إِقْبَالِكُمْ

O members of the Muḥammadan household
happiness is in your approach

مُنُّوا عَلَيَّ بِنَظْرَةٍ

تُحْيِي الفُؤَادَ بِسِرِّكُمْ

Grace me with a glance
enlivening the heart by your secret

وَ أَحِبَّتِي يَا سَادَتِي

الكُلُّ يَحْضُرُ عِنْدَكُمْ

My beloved, O my masters!
Everyone arrives with you

بِيْضُ الوُجُوهِ ضِيَاؤُكُمْ

يُضْوِى فُؤَادَ مُحِبِّكُمْ

Radiant faces, your light
illumines the heart of your lovers

إِشْرَاقُ نُورٍ مِنْكُمُ

كَالشَّمْسِ يُظْهِرُ فَضْلَكُمْ

A light from you shining
like the sun disclosing your virtue

مَا خَابَ عَبْدٌ زَارَكُمْ

وَ أَتَى المَقَامَ بِحُبِّكُمْ

No slave visiting you is disappointed
none who come to the maqam loving you

يَرْجُو الرِّضَا مِنْ أَحْمَدٍ

خَيْرِ الخَلِيقَةِ جَدِّكُمْ

Hoping for satisfaction from Aḥmad
the best of creation, your Grandfather

فَبِجَاهِهِ وَ بِحُبِّهِ

أَرْجُو الرِّضَا مِنْ عَطْفِكُمْ

By his glory and by love for him
I hope for pleasure from your affection

أَسْتَغْفِرُ اللّٰهَ الَّذِى
عَمَرَ الوُجُودَ بِعِلْمِكُمْ

I seek forgiveness from Allah Who
made existence flourish by your knowledge

يَا أَهْلَ عِلْمٍ نَافِعٍ
نَفَعَ الخَلَائِقَ قَوْلُكُمْ

O people of beneficial knowledge
your statements benefit creation

مِنْ أَحْمَدٍ خَيْرِ الوَرَى
جِئْتُمْ وَ شَعَّ ضِيَاؤُكُمْ

From Aḥmad, the best of creation,
you came, and your light radiated

مَنْ مِثْلُكُمْ فِي عِزِّكُمْ
اللّٰهُ أَظْهَرَ عِزَّكُمْ

Who is like you, in your glory
Allah has manifested your glory

أَلْقَى عَلَيْكُمْ حُبَّهُ
كُلُّ القُلُوبِ تُحِبُّكُمْ

He cast His love upon you
all the hearts love you

سُبْحَانَ رَبِّي إِنَّهُ

بِالطُّهْرِ طَهَّرَ بَيْتَكُمْ

Glory to my Lord, He
purified your household with chastity,

عَمَّ الأَنَامَ بِرَحْمَةٍ

يَا رَحْمَةً مِنْ رَبِّكُمْ

Enveloped humanity with mercy
O Mercy from your Lord!

يَا بَضْعَةً مِنْ أَحْمَدٍ

أَنْتُمْ سُلَالَةُ جَدِّكُمْ

O you, portion from Aḥmad!
You are the progeny of your Grandfather

يَا آلَ بَيْتِ مُحَمَّدٍ

كُلُّ القُلُوبِ تَوَدُّكُمْ

O members of the Muḥammadan household
all the hearts have for you affection

الحُبُّ فَرْضٌ لَازِمٌ

يَا سَعْدَ أَهْلِ وِدَادِكُمْ

Love is a binding obligation
how fortunate those devoted to your affection!

اللَّهُ يَمْنَحُنِي الهُدَى

بِوِدَادِكُمْ مِنْ أَجْلِكُمْ

Allah regales me with guidance
by love for you, for your sake

يَهْدِي لِرُوحِي دَايِماً

لَا تَنْثَنِي عَنْ نَهْجِكُمْ

He guides my soul always
do not divert me from your methodology

أَتْلُو الكِتَابَ مُرَتِّلاً

لَا سِيَّما بِضَرِيحِكُمْ

I recite the Book gracefully
especially by your grave

فِيهَ التَّجَلِّي وَ الهُدَى

مِنْ خَيْرِ فَضْلِ مَلِيكِكُمْ

In it are manifestations and guidance
from the good favor of your King

اللَّهُ رَبِّي قَدْ هَدَى

عَبْداً أَتَى فِي دَارِكُمْ

Allah, my Lord, has indeed guided
a slave who came to your abode

يُقْرِى السَّلَامَ عَلَيْكُمُ

عِنْدَ المَقَامِ مَقَامِكُمْ

He extends to you the greeting
at the maqam, your maqam

فِيهِ الضِّيَا مِنْ نُورِكُمْ

جَاءَ النَّسِيمُ بِعِطْرِكُمْ

In it is radiance from your light
a fresh breeze comes with your fragrance

فَرِحَ الفُؤَادُ بِحُبِّكُمْ

يَا مَرْحَباً بِنَسِيمِكُمْ

With love for you the heart rejoices
welcome to your pleasant breeze!

المِسْكُ فَاحَ لِزَائِرٍ

نَشْوَانَ يَنْشَقُ عَرْفَكُمْ

Musk exudes for a visitor
elated, your fragrance inhaling

جَذَبَ القُلُوبَ وِدَادُكُمْ

كُلُّ الأَنَامِ تَوَدُّكُمْ

Love for you attracts hearts,
all humans to you show affection

جَاءُوا بِحُبِّ خَالِصِ
يَدْعُونَ رَبِّي عِنْدَكُمْ

They come with love sincere
calling on my Lord in your presence

اللّٰهُ يَقْبَلُ مِنْهُمُ
دَعَوَاتِهِمْ مِنْ أَجْلِكُمْ

Allah accepts from them
their supplications, for your sake

أَيَامُكُمْ قَدْ أَشْرَقَتْ
شَمْسُ الفَضَايِلِ شَمْسُكُمْ

Your days have shone brightly
the sun of virtues is your sun

مَا كَانَ بَعْدِى عَنْ قِلًى
وَ أَنَا أُرَدِّدُ مَدْحَكُمْ

No hatred comes after me
while your eulogy I reiterate

بِاللّٰهِ أَرْجُو فَضْلَكُمْ
لَا تَحْرِمُونِي عَطْفَكُمْ

By Allah I place my hope in your virtue
do not deprive me of your sympathy!

أَرْجُو الرِّضَا يَا سَادَتِي
مِنْ نُورِ فَضْلِ دُعَايِكُمْ

I hope for pleasure, my masters
from the light of your gracious supplication

وَ صَلَاةُ رَبِّي دَايِماً
تَغْشَى النَّبِيَّ حَبِيبَكُمْ

May the prayers of my Lord always
envelop the Prophet, your Beloved

وَ كَذَا السَّلَامُ عَلَيْكُمُ
مَا فَاحَ عِطْرُ مَدِيحِكُمْ

Likewise, greetings of peace be upon you,
so long as the scent of your eulogy spreads

مَا الجَعْفَرِيُّ بِبَابِكُمْ
يَرْجُو الرِّضَا مِنْ فَضْلِكُمْ

So long as al-Jaʿfarī is by your door
hoping for pleasure through your favor

-6-

## The Light of Allah

النُّورُ لَاحَ فَأَبْكَانِي

وَ الوَجْدُ حَرَّكَ أَشْجَانِي

The light shone and made me cry,
so ecstasy stirred my sorrows

مَا كُنْتُ أَنْسَى يَا إِخْوَانِي

حُبَّ النَّبِيِّ العَدْنَانِي

I have not forgotten, O my brothers,
love for the ʿAdnānī Prophet

حُبُّ النَّبِيِّ المُبَرَّا

فِي القَلْبِ مِنِّي اسْتَقَرَّا

Love for the guiltless Prophet
in my heart is entrenched

وَ مَدْحُهُ القَلْبَ سَرَّا
مَدْحُ النَّبِيِّ النُّورَانِي

Praise for him gladdens the heart,
praise for the luminous Prophet

مَدْحُ النَّبِيِّ الأَوَّابِ
هَادٍ وَ دَاعٍ بِكِتَابِ

Praise for the oft-glorifying[27] Prophet,
guiding and calling by a Book:

قُرْآنِ رَبٍّ وَهَّابِ
فِيهِ الضِّيَاءُ الرَّبَّانِي

The Qur'ān of a Most Generous Lord,
containing Lordly light

هَذَا نَبِيُّ الحَسَنَاتِ
عَالِي المَقَامِ بِجَنَّاتِ

This is the Prophet of good deeds,
of lofty rank in the Gardens

عَرِّجْ عَلَيْهِ بِرَوْضَاتِ
وَ اقْرَا السَّلَامَ الرُّوحَانِي

Turn to him in the meadows,
convey the greeting imbued with soul

27 Oft-returning to Allah and constantly engaged in His remembrance and glorification.

هَذَا النَّبِيّ المَبْعُوثُ

رَحْمَةُ رَبِّي وَ غُيُوثُ

This sent Prophet
is the mercy of my Lord and an abundant rain[28]

جَاءَتْ إِلَيْهِ البُعُوثُ

نُورٌ لِكُلِّ الأَزْمَانِ

Delegations come to him
a light for every time

نُورُ النَّبِيّ الوَهَّاجِ

بَانَ لِكُلِّ الحُجَّاجِ

The light of the resplendent Prophet
was made clear to all the pilgrims

يَا رَبِّ عَجِّلْ إِفْرَاجِى

حَتَّى أَزُورَ كَإِخْوَانِي

My Lord, expedite my departure
that I can pay visit, like my brothers

لَيْلِي نَهَارِى وَ صَبَاحِى

أَرْجُو لِفَتْحِ الفَتَّاحِ

My night, my day, and my morning
I hope for the opening of the Opener

28 Rains that bring goodness.

يَا رَبِّ عَجِّلْ بِرَوَاحِي

نَحْوَ النَّبِيِّ المِعْوَانِ

My Lord, expedite my departure
toward the oft-succouring Prophet

نَمْشِي بِوُدٍّ وَ تَآخِي

نَنْظُرْ طَرِيقَ المَنَاخِ

By love we proceed, with mutual brotherliness,
looking at the path of the halting place

نُسْرِعْ بِغَيْرِ تَرَاخِي

نُهْدِي سَلَامَ العِرْفَانِ

Without tardiness we hasten,
conveying the peace of gnosis

هَذَا النَّبِيُّ المَحْمُودُ

شَافِعْ مُشَفَّعْ مَقْصُودُ

This praised Prophet
is an intercessor gifted intercession, sought-after,

بَرٌّ رَحِيمٌ وَ وَدُودُ

مَحْبُوبُ رَبِّ دَيَّانِ

reverent, compassionate, affectionate,
the beloved of the Lord, the Judge,

حِبٌّ مُحَبَّبْ مَبْرُورْ
هَذَا النَّبِيُّ المَنْصُورْ

Lover, endeared, accepted for grace,
this supported Prophet

يَا سَعْدَ عَبْدٍ يَزُورْ
قَبْرَ النَّبِيِّ العَدْنَانِي

How fortunate a slave who visits
the grave of the ʿAdnānī Prophet

يَا سَعْدَ عَبْدٍ يَلُوذْ
عِنْدَ المَقَامِ يَفُوزْ

How fortunate a slave taking shelter
by the maqam, victorious

يَوْمَ الصِّرَاطِ يَجُوزْ
مِنْ فَوْقِ مَتْنِ النِّيرَانِ

on the Day he crosses the Sirāt [29]
over the back of the Fires

خَيْرُ الوَرَى بَيْنَ النَّاسِ
أَغْلَى وَ أَعْلَى الأَجْنَاسِ

The best of mankind amid people
is the most precious, the loftiest of species

29 The bridge above Hell-Fire.

مَا كَانَ يَقْرَا فِي كُرَّاسِ

ذُو العِلْمِ عِلْمِ رَبَّانِي

He did not read from any booklet
possessor of knowledge, Lordly knowledge!

الحُبُّ سَارٍ وَ فَاشِي

أُنْظُرْ لِبَاكٍ وَ مَاشِي

Love pervades and permeates,
look at one weeping, and at one walking

مَا كَانَ يَسْمَعُ لِلوَاشِي

هَامَ بِحُبِّ العَدْنَانِي

Who never pays attention to slanderers,
infatuated with love for the ʿAdnānī

نَرْجُو مَنَالَ الخَلَاصِ

يَوْمَ ظُهُورِ القِصَاصِ

We hope to attain rescue
on the Day when retaliation manifests

فِي يَوْمِ أَخْذِ النَّوَاصِي

نَرْجُو الشَّفِيعَ العَدْنَانِي

On the Day when forelocks are seized,
our hope is in the ʿAdnānī intercessor

شَرَّفَ سَمَاءً وَ الأَرْضَا

أَهْدَى النَّوَافِلَ وَ الفَرْضَا

Who ennobled the sky and the earth
offering voluntary and compulsory prayers

سَنَّ التَّعَاوُنَ وَ القَرْضَا

أَعْلَى الوَرَى فِي الإِيمَانِ

He instituted cooperation and loans
the highest of creatures in īmān

صَلَّى العَلِيُّ الرَّحْمَنُ

رَبُّ العِبَادِ الدَّيَّانُ

May the Exalted, the All-Merciful,
the Lord-King of servants,

خَيْرَ الصَّلَاةِ وَ تَزْدَانُ

لِلهَاشِمِيِّ العَدْنَانِي

Send the best of prayers, graced
on the Hāshimī ʿAdnānī

مَا الجَعْفَرِيُّ قَالَ الدُّرَرَا

فِي مَدْحِ مَنْ فَاقَ القَمَرَا

So long as al-Jaʿfarī utters pearls
in praise of him who surpassed the moon,

يَرْجُو الشَّفَاعَةَ وَ النَّظَرَا

مِنْ هَاشِمِيٍّ عَدْنَانِي

hoping for intercession and a look
from the Hāshimī ʿAdnānī

-7-

## MESSENGER OF ALLAH, I HALTED MY MOUNT

رَسُولَ اللّهِ قَدْ أَنْزَلْتُ رَحْلِي
بِبَابِكَ وَ السَّلَامُ عَلَيْكَ مِنِّي

Messenger of Allah, I halted my mount
by your door, and send greetings to you from me

لِعِلْمِي أَنَّكَ الحِصْنُ المُعَلَّى
فَنِعْمَ الحَالُ وَ المُخْتَارُ حِصْنِي

Due to my knowledge that you are the exalted fortress,
what a wonderful state when the Chosen one is my buttress

لِأَنَّكَ رَحْمَةُ الرَّحْمٰنِ عَمَّتْ
جَمِيعَ الكَوْنِ مِنْ إِنْسٍ وَ جِنِّ

As you are the mercy of the All-Merciful
encompassing all creatures, humans and jinn

وَ تَوَّجَكَ الإِلَهُ بِتَاجِ عِزٍّ
وَ إِكْرَامٍ فَيَا مَوْلَاىَ خُذْنِي

The Divine crowned you with a crown of might
and ennoblement, so my master, take me

إِلَى نُورٍ يُطَهِّرُ رَانَ قَلْبِي
وَ تَمْلَؤُهُ عُلُوماً مِنْكَ تُهْنِي

to a light which cleanses the rust of my heart
and fills it with sciences from you, made wholesome

فَأَنْتَ مَدِينَةٌ مُلِئَتْ عُلُوماً
عَلِيٌّ بَابُهَا فِي كُلِّ فَنِّ

You are a city filled with sciences
ʿAlī is its gate in every discipline

سَأَلْتُكَ عِلْمَ شَرْعِكَ يَا حَبِيبِي
فَبِالحَسَنَيْنِ وَ الزَّهْرَا أَجِبْنِي

I ask you for knowledge of your Sharīʾa, O my Beloved,
so by the two Ḥasans and the Resplendent[30] please answer me!

وَ أَمْدِدْنِي بِأَسْرَارٍ عِظَامٍ
وَ نَفْعَ المُسْلِمِينَ يَكُونُ شَأْنِي

Provide me with vast secrets
that benefiting the Muslims might be my affair

30 Al-Zahrāʾ: Sayyida Fāṭima 

بِجَاهِكَ قَدْ سَأَلْتُ اللَّهَ رَبِّي

إِجَابَةَ دَعْوَتِي وَ رِضَاهُ عَنِّي

By your rank I ask Allah, my Lord
to answer my call and be pleased with me

فَجَاهُكَ عِنْدَهُ جَاهٌ عَظِيمٌ

بِهِ فِي الحَشْرِ لِلرَّحْمٰنِ تُدْنِي

Your rank with Him is truly immense!
By it, at the Gathering[31] you are close to the All-Merciful

وَ تَشْفَعُ لِلقَضَاءِ بِيَوْمِ كَرْبٍ

لِمَنْ وَفَدُوا إِلَيْكَ بِحُسْنِ ظَنِّ

And you intercede for the judgment on the Day of Grief
for those who paid you visit having a good opinion

وَ تَكْشِفُ عَنْهُمْ كَرْباً عَظِيماً

وَ لَيْسَ سِوَاكَ يَكْشِفُهُ وَ يُثْنِي

You relieve them of a mighty sorrow
none but you dispel and divert it

لِأَنَّكَ أَكْرَمُ الأَخْيَارِ قَدْراً

حَبِيبَ اللَّهِ مِنْ عِلْمٍ أَفِدْنِي

Because you are the most noble of the chosen in rank
Beloved of Allah, redeem me by knowledge!

31 Day of Resurrection.

وَ أَيَّدَكَ الإِلَهُ بِكُلِّ خَيْرٍ

وَ قُرْآنٍ كَمِثْلِ الشَّمْسِ يُغْنِي

The Divine aided you with every good
and the Qur'ān is like a sun that enriches

فَضَايِلُهُ تَعُمُّ الكَوْنَ نُوراً

وَ إِرْشَاداً إِلَى جَنَّاتِ عَدْنِ

Its virtues envelop the cosmos with light
and is guidance towards Gardens of Eden

وَ يَشْرَحُ لِلصُّدُورِ وَ مَنْ تَلَاهُ

يَعِشْ فِي العُمْرِ مَحْفُوفاً بِأَمْنِ

The breasts it expands, and its reciter
lives engulfed in safety

يَدُومُ مُرَتَّلاً نُوراً عَلِيّاً

يُشَيِّدُ دِينَكَ العَالِي وَ يَبْنِي

Constantly recited, a light exalted,
erecting and building your lofty Dīn

أَمَانُ المُسْلِمِينَ عَظِيمُ جَاهٍ

شَفِيعٌ لِلَّذِى قَدْ كَانَ يَجْنِي

The safety of the Muslims, of glorious rank
intercessor for the one who incurs harm

$$\text{رَسُولُ اللَّهِ غَوْثٌ بَلْ غِيَاثٌ}$$
$$\text{أَزَالَ عَنِ البَرِيَّةِ كُلَّ شَيْنِ}$$

The Messenger of Allah is the Helper, rather he is aid!
Removing every blemish from humanity

$$\text{وَ نَادَتْهُ الغَزَالَةُ فِي فَلَاةٍ}$$
$$\text{أَبَا الزَّهْرَاءِ مِنْ كَرْبِي أَجِرْنِي}$$

The doe called him in the wilderness,
'Father of the Resplendent[32], relieve me from my distress'

$$\text{فَأَطْلَقَهَا النَّبِيُّ وَ كَانَ سَمْحاً}$$
$$\text{يُحَقِّقُ لِلرَّجَاءِ لِكُلِّ مُدْنِي}$$

So the Prophet freed her, tolerantly
He fulfils the hope of everyone approaching

$$\text{وَ رَوْضَتُهُ الشَّرِيفَةُ يَا أَخَانَا}$$
$$\text{تَسُرُّ القَلْبَ مِنْ هَمٍّ وَ حُزْنِ}$$

His noble Rawḍa, our brother,
gladdens the heart from worry and sorrow

$$\text{بِهَا رَوْحٌ وَ رَيْحَانٌ وَ نُورٌ}$$
$$\text{بِهَا سَعْدِي وَ إِرْشَادِي وَ يُمْنِي}$$

In it is solace, sweetness, and light
In it is my happiness, my guidance, and my success

---

32  Al-Zahrā': Sayyida Fāṭima

بِهَا الْمُخْتَارُ بَسَّاماً تَرَاهُ

يُحَيِّي الزَّائِرِينَ بِكُلِّ أَمْنِ

In it is the Chosen one, you will see him smiling,
greeting the visitors in total safety

يُبَشِّرُهُمْ بِمَا جَاءُوا إِلَيْهِ

وَ يَشْفَعُ لِلجَمِيعِ بِلاَ تَأَنِّي

He gives them glad tidings of what they came to him for
and intercedes for all without delay

عَلَيْهِ اللّٰهُ صَلَّى كُلَّ حِيْنٍ

مَعَ التَّسْلِيمِ مَا حَادٍ يُغَنِّي

On him Allah sends prayers all the time
with the greeting, so long as the cameleer chants

وَ آلٍ ثُمَّ أَصْحَابٍ كِرَامٍ

أُهَيْلِ اللّٰهِ مَنْ حَلُّوا بِعَدْنِ

On family members, then on noble Companions,
the people of Allah, those who alighted in Eden

إِلَيْكَ الجَعْفَرِيُّ أَتَى بِمَدْحٍ

رَسُولَ اللّٰهِ قَدْ أَحْسَنْتُ ظَنِّي

To you al-Jaʿfarī comes with a eulogy
Messenger of Allah, I have brought a good thought

-8-

## Did It Call You?

رَبَّنَا يَا رَبَّنَا يَا رَبَّنَا
رَبَّنَا صَلِّ عَلَى خَيْرِ الوَرَى

Our Lord, our Lord, our Lord!
Our Lord, send prayers on the best of creation

هَل دَعَاكَ الشَّوْقُ يَوْماً لِلسُّرَى
نَحْوَ بَيْتِ اللَّهِ فِي أُمِّ القُرَى

Did longing call you one day to travel
toward the House of Allah in the Mother of Cities[33]

وَ رَأَيْتَ البَيْتَ يَبْدُو نُورُهُ
مِنْ جَلَالِ اللَّهِ رَبِّي نُورَا

And you saw the light of the House emerging
from Allah, my Lord, as light?

33 Umm al-Qurā: Makka.

رَحَمَاتٌ كُلَّ يَوْمٍ عِنْدَهُ

مِنْ إِلَهِي نَازِلَاتٌ لِلْوَرَى

Copious loads of mercy each day at it
from my God descending to creation

كُلُّ مَنْ طَافَ بِهِ يَا سَعْدَهُ

غَفَرَ اللَّهُ لَهُ مَا قَدْ جَرَى

Whoever circles around it, how fortunate!
Allah forgives him for mishaps that occurred

كُلُّ رُسْلِ اللَّهِ قَدْ طَافُوا بِهِ

وَ كَذَا الأَقْطَابُ مِنْ غَيْرِ مِرَا

All the Messengers of Allah made ṭawāf around it
and so did the Poles[34], there is no doubt about it

أَحْمَدُ المُخْتَارُ قَدْ طَافَ بِهِ

شَرَّفَ البَيْتَ وَ أَطْبَاقَ الثَّرَى

Aḥmad the Chosen one made ṭawāf around it
he honored the House and the layers of ground

كَانَ كَالشَّمْسِ إِذَا دَارَتْ عَلَى

فَلَكَ الدُّنْيَا لَدَى الكُلِّ تُرَى

He was like the sun when it revolves
its celestial orbit for all to see

34 Qutb pl. aqtab: a person of the highest spiritual rank.

كَانَ كَالبَدْرِ إِذَا عَمَّ السَّمَا
وَ بِقَاعَ الأَرْضِ نُوراً أَقْمَرَا

He was like the moon when it pervades the sky
the surface of the Earth moonlit by his light

لَيْتَنِي شَاهَدْتَهُ فِي مَشْيِهِ
حَوْلَ بَيْتِ اللَّهِ مَرْفُوعَ الذَّرَى

Would that I had witnessed him walking!
around the House of Allah, elevated in knowledge

لِلَثَمْتُ الأَرْضَ تَكْرِيماً لَهُ
وَ شَمَمْتُ التُّرْبَ مِنْهَا عَنْبَرَا

So I could have kissed the ground out of honor for him
And sniffed the dust from which comes the scent of ambergris

لَيْتَنِي شَاهَدْتُهُ فِي جِلْسَةِ
تُدْهِشُ الشَّمْسَ لَدَى غَارِ حِرَا

Would that I had witnessed him sitting
bewildering the Sun in the Cave of Hira

لِرَأَيْتُ الغَارَ فِي عَلْيَائِهِ
فَلَكُ الشَّمْسِ إِذَا الهَادِي قَرَا

So I could have seen the cave in its loftiness
the orbit of the Sun when the Guide reads

لَيْتَنِي شَاهَدْتُهُ حِيْنَ أَتَى
زَمْزَمَ الشُّرْبِ لَخِلْتُ الكَوْثَرَا

Would that I had witnessed when he came
I would regard the drinking of Zamzam to be as al-Kawthar

شَرَّفَ الأَسْعَدَ فِي تَقْبِيلِهِ
أَكْرَمَ اللَّهُ بِهِ ذَا الحَجَرَا

He honored the Black stone by kissing it
Thus, Allah ennobled by him the possessor of the stone[35]

تَتَمَنَّى الخُلْدُ أَنْ تَحْظَى بِمَا
حَظِيَ الأَسْعَدُ فِيمَا قَدْ جَرَى

Everlastingness wishes to enjoy
what the most fortunate relished in what is bygone

ضَمَّ لِلْكَعْبَةِ حُبًّا فَعْلاً
قَدْرُهَا بِالمُصْطَفَى خَيْرِ الوَرَى

He attached to the Ka'ba an active love
its rank is by the Chosen one, the best of creatures

وَ رَأَيْتُ القَومَ سَارُوا نَحْوَهُ
رَاكِبِينَ الخَيْلَ قَدْ حَثُّوا السُّرَى

I saw the people heading for him
riding horses, hastening the travel

35 The Ka'ba

كُلَّمَا لَاحَ لَهُمْ بَرْقُ السَّمَا
ذَكَرُوا النُّورَ البَهِيَّ الأَقْمَرَا

Whenever the lightning of the sky shone to them,
they remembered the radiant moonlit glow

نُورَ خَيْرِ الخَلْقِ مَنْ جَاءُوا لَهُ
تَارِكِينَ الأَهْلَ شَوْقاً وَ القُرَى

The light of the best of creation they came for
leaving behind family and villages, longingly

كُلَّمَا هَبَّتْ لَهُمْ رِيحُ الصَّبَا
أَهْدَتِ العِطْرَ الذَّكِيَّ العَنْبَرَا

Whenever the east wind blows for them,
it brings the pleasant scent of ambergris

رَوَّحَتْ أَرْوَاحَهُمْ مِمَّا بِهَا
وَ رَأَوْا نُوراً جَمِيلاً أَخْضَرا

Relieving their souls of every burden,
so they saw a lovely green light

يَشْرَحُ الصَّدْرَ إِذَا مَا خِلْتَهُ
وَ يُنَادِي كُلَّ قَلْبٍ عُمِّرَا

Expanding the breast when you conceive it
and summoning every enlivened heart

صَلَوَاتُ اللّٰهِ تَغْشَى دَايِماً
ذَلِكَ الوَجْهَ الكَرِيمَ الأَنْوَرَا

The prayers of Allah always engulf
that noble, brightest face

جَعْفَرِيُّ الأَصْلِ يَدْعُو قَايِلاً
هَلْ دَعَاكَ الشَّوْقُ يَوْماً لِلسُّرَى

Jaʿfarī by descent invokes thus saying:
Has longing called you one day to travel?

-9-

## The Ship of the Folk

هَلْ تَعْرِفُ الشِّرْبَ يَا هَذَا وَ دَوْلَتَهُ
أَوْ كُنْتَ تَدْرِى الَّذِى بِالحُبِّ قَدْ سَكِرَا

Do you know the drink, O poor soul, and its being passed around?
Or do you know the one inebriated by love?

مَا كَانَ ذَا الخَمْرُ مَجْعُولاً لِمَنْ رَقَدُوا
بَلْ كَانَ ذَا الشِّرْبُ مَجْعُولاً لِمَنْ سَهِرَا

The wine is not laid for those who sleep
rather the drink is set for him who keeps vigil!

فَإِنْ شَرِبْتَ شَرَابَ العَارِفِينَ لَهُ
أَصْبَحْتَ فِي الكَوْنِ سُلْطَاناً وَ مُنْتَصِرَا

If you drink the beverage of the Gnostics
you will become a Sultan of creation, victorious

وَ إِنْ رَكَنْتَ إِلَى الدُّنْيَا وَ زِينَتِهَا
أَصْبَحْتَ عَبْداً لَهَا كَالكَلْبِ مُنْزَجِرَا

If on this world you lean, and on its ornament,
you will be enslaved to it, like a dog scolded

وَ إِنْ نَظَرْتَ إِلَى خَلْقٍ فَأَنْتَ لَهُمْ
وَ هُمْ حِجَابُكَ حَتَّى تُبْصِرَ القَمَرَا

If you look to creation, you are one of them
they are your veil until you see the moon

وَ إِنْ رَكِبْتَ لَدَى بَحْرٍ سَفِينَتَهُمْ
فَلَازِمِ الصَّمْتَ حَتَّى تَعْرِفَ الخَبَرَا

If on a sea, you board their ship,
cling to silence until you learn the news

وَ إِنْ مَشَيْتَ مَعَ الأَحْبَابِ تَخْدُمُهُمْ
لَا بُدَّ مِنْ يَومٍ خَيْرٍ تُبْصِرُ الخَضِرَا

If you walk with the lovers, you should serve them
there is no escaping the best day when you see al-Khaḍir

يَخْضَرُّ زَرْعُكَ بَعْدَ اليُبْسِ تُبْصِرُهُ
وَ بِالتَّوَاضُعِ يَأْتِي الغَيْثُ مُنْحَدِرَا

Your crop will flourish after dryness, this will be visible
copious rain will come due to humility

وَ اقْتُلْ غَلَاماً لِنَفْسِ السُّوْءِ يَأْمُرُهَا
سُوْءاً وَ كُنْ ذَاكِراً تُهْدَى كَمَنْ ذَكَرَا

Slay a boy[36] , the evil ego commands to evil
be a person of dhikr and you will be guided like its adepts

أَقِمْ جِدَارَكَ فِي جِدٍّ وَ فِي عَمَلٍ
فَالكَنْزُ مِنْ بَعْدِ جِدٍّ تَلْقَهُ حَضَرَا

Straighten your wall[37], earnestly and diligently
the treasure[38], after an effort you will receive it openly

فَإِنْ أَرَدْتَ كَرَامَاتٍ لِتَعْرِفَهَا
فَاتْبَعْ أُخَيَّ طَرِيقَ القَوْمِ وَ الأَثَرَا

If you want preternatural events that you recognize
then follow, my brother, the path of the Folk, and their footprints

وَ ارْكَبْ سَفِينَتَهُمْ تَعْرِفْ خَوَارِقَهُمْ
تَجْرِى السَّفِينَةُ مِنْ بَعْدِ الَّذِى كُسِرَا

Embark on their ship, you will learn their norm-breaking,
the ship will sail after the one that is smashed

36 Reference to the encounter between Sayyidunā Mūsā and al-Khiḍr ﷺ, see Qur'ān 18:65
37 Reference to the encounter between Sayyidunā Mūsā and al-Khiḍr ﷺ, see Qur'ān 18:77
38 Reference to the encounter between Sayyidunā Mūsā and al-Khiḍr ﷺ, see Qur'ān 18:82

مِنْ غَيْرِ أَجْرٍ تَرَى الأَيَامَ خَادِمَةً
مِنْ أَجْلِ شَيْخِكَ لَمْ تَدْفَعْ لَهُمْ دُرَرَا

For no fee, you will see the days as service
because of your shaykh, you paid no pearls to them

لِأَنَّهُمْ يَعْرِفُونَ الشَّيْخَ مِنْ زَمَنٍ
وَ أَنْتَ ضَيْفٌ لِشَيْخٍ يَعْرِفُ الأُمَرَا

For long have they in fact known the guide
and you are a guest of a guide who knows his business

بِهِ نَجَوْتَ فَلَا أَجْرٌ وَ لَا غَرَقٌ
وَ قَدْ رَأَيْتَ مِنَ الأَحْوَالِ مَا نَدَرَا

By him you are saved, so no fee and no drowning
you see rarities of spiritual states

وَ الصَّبْرُ غَايَةُ مَا تَبْغِيهِ مِنْ أَمَلٍ
لَنْ يَعْرِفَ القَوْمَ مَنْ لَمْ يَعْرِفْ الصَّبْرَا

Patience is your utmost hope
no one disowning patience will ever know the Folk

العِلْمِ عِنْدَهُمُ الرُّشْدُ حَالُهُمُ
فَاخْضَعْ خُضُوعاً تَرَى مَا كَانَ مُسْتَتِرَا

Knowledge is with them, their state is right guidance
submit then, and you will see what lay hidden

سَلِّمْ لَهُمْ حَالَهُمْ حَتَّى تَكُونَ عَلَى
حَالٍ تَرَى حَالَهُمْ سَلِّمْ لِمَنْ غَبَرَا

Submit to their state until yours allows
you to perceive theirs. Submit to those who surpass

وَ الْمُنْكِرُونَ لِأَهْلِ اللَّهِ قَدْ قَفَلُوا
بَابَ الطَّرِيقِ عَلَيْهِمْ ضَيَّعُوا الأَثَرَا

Deniers of the people of Allah have locked
the door of the path on themselves, losing the traces

مَنْ جَاءَ يَبْغِي طَرِيقَ اللَّهِ يَعْبُرُهُ
مِنْ غَيْرِ هَادٍ لَهُ مَا كَانَ مُنْتَصِرَا

Whoever comes seeking the path of Allah to cross it
without a guide, he will never be successful!

كَيْفَ المَسِيرُ وَ لَمْ تَعْرِفْ مَسَالِكَهَا
قَدْ ضَلَّ سَعْيُكَ يَا هَذَا فَكُنْ حَذِرَا

How can he travel, and its routes are unfamiliar?
His effort is in vain, O poor soul, so tread cautiously

فَاتْبَعْ طَرِيقَةَ أَهْلِ اللَّهِ خَالِصَةً
خَلْفَ الإِمَامِ تَرَى أَتْبَاعَهُ زُمَرَا

Follow the pure path of the people of Allah
behind the Imām, you will see his followers in a multitude

لِكُلِّ قَوْمٍ إِمَامٌ يَقْتَدُونَ بِهِ
فَاجْعَلْ إِمَامَكَ شَيْخاً لِلعُلُومِ قَرَا

Every People has an Imām they emulate,
so make your Imām a guide, imparting sciences

طَرِيقَةُ القَوْمِ قُرْآنٌ وَ سُنَّةُ مَنْ
أَهْدَى السَّبِيلَ وَ أَحْكَاماً هُنَاكَ تُرَى

The Path of the Folk is Qur'ān and the Sunna of the one
who conveys the way and judgments, there you are shown

لَمْ يَخْرُجُوا عَنْ كِتَابِ اللَّهِ فِي عَمَلٍ
وَ لَا مَقَالٍ وَ كُلٌّ قَلْبُهُ عَمَرَا

They did not deviate from the Book of Allah in deeds
or in their words. The hearts of all of them bloomed

إِنْ جِئْتَ عِنْدَهُمُ تَلْقَ الضِّيَاءَ بِهِمْ
وَ النُّورُ لَاحَ لِمَنْ بِاللَّيْلِ قَدْ سَهِرَا

If you come to them, you are met with light from them,
light shines on the one who spends the night awake

وَ القَلْبُ يَفْرَحُ مِنْ رُؤْيَا وُجُوهِهِمُ
وَ كُلُّ مَنْ جَاءَهُمْ لَا شَكَّ قَدْ أُجِرَا

The heart rejoices on seeing their faces
whoever comes to them is no doubt rewarded

حُرَّاسُ دَوْلَتِهِ أَرْبَابُ سَطْوَتِهِ
الكَوْنُ قَدْ صَارَ مِنْ أَنْفَاسِهِمْ عَطِرَا

Guardians of His Kingdom, endowed with His authority,
the universe, by their breaths, is perfumed

فَهُمْ عَبِيدٌ وَ أَهْلُ المُلْكِ تَخْدُمُهُمْ
أَلْقَى عَلَيْهِمْ قُبُولاً مِنْهُ مُعْتَبِرَا

They are slaves, yet they are served by sovereigns
He cast on them acceptance, as an honor

اللّٰهُ يَذْكُرُهُمْ ذِكْراً يُكَرِّمُهُمْ
بَيْنَ المَلَائِكِ يَا سَعْدَ الَّذِى ذُكِرَا

Allah remembers and honors them with a remembrance
among the angels, how fortunate the ones remembered!

وَ الحَمْدُ لِلَّهِ نَالَ القَلْبُ بُغْيَتَهُ
فَالعَبْدُ عِنْدَ رَسُولِ اللَّهِ قَدْ حَضَرَا

Praise belongs to Allah, the heart reaps its desire
the slave arrives to the presence of the Messenger of Allah

وَ شَاهَدَ القُبَّةَ الخَضْرَاءَ بَادِيَةً
تُبْدِى نِدَاءً وَ تَسْلِيماً لِمَنْ عَبَرَا

He witnesses the green dome patently,
disclosing an invitation and a greeting to the wanderer

وَ رَوْضَةُ الحُبِّ بِالأَعْطَارِ عَابِقَةٌ
تُحْيِي الفُؤَادَ الَّذِى مِنْ ذَنْبِهِ دَثَرَا

The Rawḍa of love with its lingering fragrance
it gives life to the heart which effaces its sin

طُوبَى لِعَبْدٍ أَتَاهَا بَاكِياً وَجِلاً
أَهْدَى السَّلَامَ لِطَهَ فِي الدُّجَى سَحَرَا

Blessedness for a slave who comes weeping and fearful
conveying greetings to ṬāHā in the darkness of pre-dawn

وَ قَالَ يَا خَيْرَ خَلْقِ اللّهِ خُذْ بِيَدِى
عَبْدٌ أَتَاكَ بِذَنْبٍ حَيَّرَ الفِكَرَا

He says, 'O best of Allah's creation, take my hand!
A sinful slave, bewildered, has come to you

أَنْتَ الشَّفِيعُ بِيَوْمِ الحَشْرِ إِنْ وَقَفَتْ
أَهْلُ الشَّفَاعَاتِ كُلٌّ قَدَّمَ العُذُرَا

You are the intercessor on the Day of Gathering
when all intercessors hold back, tendering excuses

عَلَيْكَ صَلَّى إِلَهُ العَرْشِ مَا طَلَعَتْ
شَمْسُ السَّمَاءِ وَ نُورُ اللّهِ قَدْ ظَهَرَا

May the God of the Throne send prayers on you as long
as the sun rises in the sky and the light of Allah manifests

مَا الجَعْفَرِيُّ أَتَى بِالمَدْحِ مُبْتَهِلاً
أَهْدَى السَّلَامَ لِطَهَ فِي الدُّجَى سَحَرَا

As long as al-Jaʿfarī humbly weaves a eulogy
conveying greetings to ṬāHā in the darkness of pre-dawn'

## -10-

## Drink

شَرَابُ الرَّاحِ فِي الذِّكْرِ
شَرَابٌ فَايِحُ العِطْرِ

Drinking wine is in His remembrance
a drink of diffused fragrance

دَخَلْنَا حَضْرَةَ القُدْسِ
وَ كَانَتْ لَيْلَةَ القَدْرِ

We entered the Presence of Purity
and it was the Night of the High Rank[39]

شَرِبْنَا شَرْبَةَ الحُبِّ
وَ كَانَتْ سَاعَةَ العَصْرِ

We drank the drink of love
and it was the time of 'Asr

39 Laylat al-Qadr

شَرَاباً طَيِّبَ العَصْرِ
فَهِمْنَا طِيلَةَ العُمْرِ

A nicely squeezed beverage
we understood throughout the lifetime

بِجَوْفِ اللَّيْلِ نَادَانَا
إِلَهُ العَرْشِ لِلْفَجْرِ

In the middle of the night we invoked
the God of the Throne until dawn

فَكَمْ مِنْ سَاهِرٍ يَدْعُو
وَ كَمْ مِنْ تَالٍ لِلذِّكْرِ

How many a sleepless person invokes
and how many recites the Dhikr[40]

وَ كَمْ مِنْ قَايِمٍ يَبْكِي
بِدَمْعٍ سَالَ كَالقَطْرِ

How many a person standing weeps
with tears like raindrops falling

فَسَلْ عَنْهُ رُكَيْعَاتٍ
بِوَقْتِ اللَّيْلِ إِذْ يَسْرِى

Ask Him through some units of prayer[41]
sometime in the night, when it covers

40 The Qur'ān.
41 Raka'āt.

وَ كَمْ فِي مَسْجِدٍ عَاكِفْ

كَمِثْلِ الطَّيْرِ فِي الوَكْرِ

How many a person clings to the masjid
as if a bird perched in his nest

وَ كَمْ مِنْ بَايِعٍ شَارٍ

وَ حُبُّ القَلْبِ كَالجَمْرِ

How many a vendor purchasing
while the love of the heart is [burning] like embers

وَ كَمْ مِنْ عَابِدٍ يَمْشِي

مَعَ الأَقْطَابِ وَ الخِضْرِ

How many a worshipper walks
with the Poles and al-Khiḍr

وَ كَمْ مِنْ سَايِحٍ يَسْعَى

كَسَعْيِ الطَّيْرِ وَ النَّسْرِ

How many a roamer moves quickly
as birds and eagles speed

وَ كَمْ مِنْ عَالِمٍ يُهْدِى

لِآلِي العِلْمِ كَالبَحْرِ

How many scholars guide
to the pearls of knowledge, like the ocean

وَ كَمْ مِنْ ذَاكِرٍ لَيْلاً
كَمِثْلِ اللَّيْثِ فِي الزَّأْرِ

How many a devotee of remembrance at night
as if a lion when roaring

وَ كَمْ مِنْ صَامِتٍ يَتْلُو
بِرُوحٍ مِنْهُ فِي السِّرِّ

How many a silent person recites
with a soul from Him in secret.

## -11-

## Welcome!

أَهْلاً وَسَهْلاً بِالنَّبِي

أَهْلاً وَسَهْلاً بِالنَّبِي

Welcome to the Prophet!
Welcome to the Prophet!

أَهْلاً وَسَهْلاً بِالنَّبِي

خَيْرِ الأَنَامِ العَرَبِي

Welcome to the Prophet!
The best of mankind, the Arab

أَهْلاً وَسَهْلاً بِالحَبِيبْ

خَيْرِ الأَنَامِ نِعْمَ الطَّبِيبْ

Welcome to the Beloved!
The best of mankind, what a wonderful healer!

يامُفْرِحَ القَلْبِ الكَئِيبْ

خَيْرُ الأَنَامِ العَرَبِي

O delighter of the gloomy heart!
The best of mankind, the Arab

أَهْلاً وَسَهْلاً بِالإِمَامْ

قَدْ فَاقَ بَدْراً فِي التَّمَامْ

Welcome to the leader!
He surpasses the full moon in perfection

وَ شَفِيعُنَا يَوْمَ الزِّحَامْ

خَيْرِ الأَنَامِ العَرَبِي

Our intercessor on the Day of Crowding[42]
the best of mankind, the Arab

أَهْلاً وَسَهْلاً بِالرَّسُولْ

بَابِ الرِّضَا بَابِ القَبُولْ

Welcome to the Messenger!
The door of pleasure, the door of acceptance

وَ حُبُّهُ عَيْنُ الوُصُولْ

خَيْرِ الأَنَامِ العَرَبِي

Love for him is the source of arrival
the best of mankind, the Arab

42 Day of Resurrection.

أَهْلاً وَسَهْلاً بِالكَفِيلْ

عَالِي المَقَامِ بِلَا مَثِيلْ

Welcome to the guarantor!
Of lofty station, unparalleled

قَدْ حَلَّ فِي دَارِ النَّخِيلْ

خَيْرُ الأَنَامِ العَرَبِي

He settled in the abode of palm-trees
the best of mankind, the Arab

يَا رَوْضَةً فِيهَا الرِّضَا

وَ العَفْوُ عَمَّا قَدْ مَضَى

O Rawḍa, in it is satisfaction
and pardon for what has passed

فِيهَا النَّبِيُّ المُرْتَضَى

خَيْرُ الأَنَامِ العَرَبِي

Therein is the Prophet, al-Murtaḍā
the best of mankind, the Arab

فِيهَا الوِصَالْ فِيهَا الشُّهُودْ

فِيهَا الرُّكُوعْ فِيهَا السُّجُودْ

Therein is the connection, therein is the witnessing
therein is the bowing, therein the prostration

جَاءَتْ لَهُ خَيْرُ الوُفُودْ

خَيْرُ الأَنَامِ العَرَبِي

The best delegations came to him
the best of mankind, the Arab

بَدْرٌ إِذَا كَشَفَ اللِّثَامْ

فَازُوا بِزَوْرَتِهِ الكِرَامْ

A full moon when the veil is lifted
the noble are victorious by visiting him

وَ لَهُ التَّهَجُّدُ فِي الظَّلَامْ

خَيْرُ الأَنَامِ العَرَبِي

He prayed in the darkness of the night
the best of mankind, the Arab

وَ الكِتَابَ مُرَتِّلاً

وَ مُبَيِّناً وَ مُفَصِّلاً

He recited the Book slowly
explaining and detailing

لِلْخَلْقِ حَقاً أُرْسِلاَ

خَيْرُ الأَنَامِ العَرَبِي

Truly to [the whole] creation he was sent
the best of mankind, the Arab

شَرَّفْتَ مَكَّةَ وَ الحَرَمْ
وَ الحِجْرَ ثُمَّ المُلْتَزَمْ

Makka you ennobled, and the Ḥaram,
the Ḥijr, then the Multazam

قَدْ كُنْتَ نُوراً فِي القِدَمْ
شَرَّفْتَ كُلَّ العَرَبِي

You were light in pre-existence
you ennobled all the Arabs

بِالسَّيْفِ جِئْتَ وَبِالقَلَمْ
وَ دَعَوْتَ قَوْمَكَ لِلسَّلَمْ

With a sword you came, and with a pen
calling your people to safety

لَكَ أُمَّةٌ خَيْرُ الأُمَمْ
فِيهَا النَّبِيُّ العَرَبِي

Yours is a nation, the best of nations
wherein is the Arab Prophet

صَلَّيْتَ نَحْوَ القِبْلَتَيْنْ
جَدَّ الحَسَنْ وَ كَذا الحُسَيْنْ

You prayed in the two directions
Grandfather of al-Ḥasan, and al-Ḥusayn, too

وَ أَزَلْتَ عَنَّا كُلَّ شَيْنْ

أَنْتَ النَّبِيُّ العَرَبِي

Every disgrace you removed from us
you are the Arab Prophet

يَا صَادِقَ الوَعْدِ المُجِيرْ

أَنْتَ البَشِيرُ كَذَا النَّذِيرِ

O protector of truthful promise!
You are the bringer of glad tidings, the warner

وَ كَذَا السِّرَاجُ لَنَا المُنِيرْ

خَيْرُ الأَنَامِ العَرَبِي

Also an illuminating lamp for us
the best of mankind, the Arab

وَ بِكَ النَّجَاةُ لِمَنْ لَجَا

أَنْتَ الشَّفِيعُ المُرْتَجَى

From you is rescue for the refugee
you are the hoped-for intercessor

قَلْبٌ أَحَبَّكَ قَدْ نَجَا

وَ الحُبُّ خَيْرُ القُرَبِ

A heart that loves you finds salvation
love is the best form of nearness

قَلْبٌ أَحَبَّ المُصْطَفَى

يَلْقَى السَّعَادَةَ وَ الصَّفَا

A heart that loves the Chosen one
receives felicity and purity

إِشْفَعْ لِعَبْدٍ قَدْ هَفَا

أَنْتَ النَّبِيُّ العَرَبِي

Intercede for a slave who has slipped
you are the Arab Prophet

قَلْبٌ أَحَبَّكَ يَنْشَرِحْ

وَ الحَالُ يَزْهُو وَ يَنْصَلِحْ

A heart that loves you is expanded
while the state blossoms and improves

قَلْبُ المُحِبِّ هُوَ الفَرِحْ

بِشُهُودِ خَيْرِ العَرَبِ

The heart of the lover is in joy
by witnessing the best of the Arabs

نَادَتْ عَلَيْهِ غَزَالَةٌ

وَ لَهَا لَدَيْهِ مَقَالَةٌ

A gazelle called out to him
uttering to him a speech

فَأَتَتْهَا مِنْهُ كَفَالَةٌ

خَيْرُ الأَنَامِ العَرَبِي

And she took from him a guarantee
the best of mankind, the Arab

وَ الذِّئْبُ فِي الجَبَلْ

لِلرَّاعِي لَمَّا عَنْهُ حَلْ

And the wolf on the mountain
[spoke] to the shepherd when he prevented it from

شَاةً كَذَا لِلرَّاعِي دَلْ

عَلَى خِيَارِ العَرَبِ

A sheep, so the shepherd was guided
to the choicest among the Arabs

فِي الصَّخْرِ غَاصَ لَهُ القَدَمْ

فِي الرَّمْلِ لَمْ يَظْهَرْ وَلَمْ

On the rock his feet was immersed
[yet] in the sand, it neither imprinted nor

يَثْقُلْ عَلَيْهَا المُحْتَرَمْ

خَيْرُ الأَنَامِ العَرَبِي

Weighed heavily on it, the honored-being
the best of mankind, the Arab

جَاءَ الحَدِيثُ المُشْتَهَرْ
لِلْهَادِى قَدْ سَعَتِ الشَّجَرْ

The widespread Ḥadith came
that to the Guide the trees hastened

لَمَّا دَعَاهَا بِهَا اسْتَتَرْ
خَيْرُ الأَنَامِ العَرَبِي

When he summoned them, to take them as a barrier
the best of mankind, the Arab

وَ الضَّبُّ يَشْهَدُ بِالكَلَامِ
لِلمُصْطَفَى خَيْرِ الأَنَامْ

The lizard bore witness with [clear] speech
to the Chosen one, the best of humans

وَ بِأَنَّهُ بَدْرُ الخِتَامْ
خَيْرُ الأَنَامِ العَرَبِي

And he is the full moon, the seal
the best of mankind, the Arab

وَ البِئْرُ مَالِحُ مَاؤُهَا
بِالرِّيقِ يَعْذُبُ مَلْحُهَا

The well of salty waters
by his saliva turn into a spring of sweetness

عَذْبٌ فُرَاتٌ شَرَابُهَا

مِنْ رِيقِ خَيْرِ العَرَبِ

Fresh and sweet its drink
from the saliva of the best of Arabs

لِلعَرْشِ حَقًّا قَدْ وَصَلْ

خَيْرَ المَنَازِلِ قَدْ نَزَلْ

Truly the Throne he reached
the best of stations he alighted

قَدْ شَاهَدَ المَوْلَى الأَجَلْ

خَيْرُ الأَنَامِ العَرَبِي

He witnessed the Most Majestic Master,
the best of mankind, the Arab

وَ أَتَى بِخَمْسٍ إِنَّهَا

خَيْرٌ وَ نُورٌ كُلُّهَا

He brought five [prayers]
all of them are goodness and light

خَيْرُ الفَضَايِلِ فَضْلُهَا

مِنْ أَجْلِ خَيْرِ العَرَبِ

The greatest of virtue is their virtue
for the sake of the best of Arabs

وَ تَشَرَّفَتْ مِنْهُ الطِّبَاقْ
بَدْرُ التَّمَامِ بِلَا مُحَاقْ

By him generations were honored
the perfect full moon without waning

بِالصُّلْحِ جَاءَ وَ بِالوِفَاقْ
خَيْرُ الأَنَامِ العَرَبِي

With reconciliation and harmony he came
the best of mankind, the Arab

بِالبَيْتِ طَافَ مُهَرْوِلَا
لِلرُّكْنِ صَارَ مُقَبِّلَا

They make ṭawāf of the House at a quick pace
heading for the corner, to kiss

لِلكُفْرِ جَاءَ مُعَطِّلَا
خَيْرُ الأَنَامِ العَرَبِي

He came to nullify disbelief
the best of mankind, the Arab

نَطَقَ المَسِيحُ بِإِسْمِهِ
وَ بِوَصْفِهِ وَ بِعِلْمِهِ

The Messiah verbalized his name,
his description and his knowledge

فَاقَ الوَرَى فِي حِلْمِهِ

خَيْرُ الأَنَامِ العَرَبِي

He surpassed all mankind in clemency
the best of mankind, the Arab

تَوْرَاةُ مُوسَى قَدْ ذَكَرْ

وَصْفَ النَّبِيِّ المُشْتَهَرْ

The Torah of Mūsā made mention
of the description of the well-known Prophet

مَنْ نُورُهُ فَاقَ القَمَرْ

خَيْرُ الأَنَامِ العَرَبِي

In his light he outshone the moon
the best of mankind, the Arab

وَ الجِذْعِ يَبْكِي لَهُ أَنِينْ

لِلمُصْطَفَى الهَادِى الأَمِينْ

The trunk wept with a lamentation
for the Chosen Guide, the Trustworthy

شَوْقاً لَهُ يَا سَامِعِينْ

خَيْرُ الأَنَامِ العَرَبِي

Yearning for him, O listeners
the best of mankind, the Arab

طَيْرُ الفَلَاةُ تَوَسَّلَا
وَ إِلَيْهِ جَاءَ وَ أَقْبَلَا

The birds in the desert sought his mediation
to Him they came, approaching

وَ جَنَاحَهُ قَدْ أَرْسَلَا
نَحْوَ النَّبِيِّ العَرَبِي

Their wings they spread loose
towards the Arab Prophet

وَ المَاءُ مِنْ كَفٍّ لَقَدْ
أَرْوَى لِجَيْشٍ ذِى رَشَدْ

The water from his palm
quenched the rightly-guided army's thirst

شَرِبُوا مِنَ الهَادِى المَدَدْ
خَيْرِ الأَنَامِ العَرَبِي

They drank from the support of the Guide
the best of mankind, the Arab

بَارَكْ لِجَابِرِ فِى العَنَاقْ
وَ طَعَامِهِ وَ الجَيْشَ سَاقْ

Jābir was blessed in his she-kid
and in his food[43], giving the soldiers to drink[44]

43 Ṣaḥīḥ al-Bukhārī 4101.
44 Sayyiduna Jābir b. ʿAbd Allāh served the thirsty soldiers during the Battle of Uḥud.

لِلْبَيْتِ مَأْمُونَ المَحَاقْ

بِالهَاشِمِيِّ العَرَبِي

For the House, safe from waning
by the Hāshimī Arab

وَ بِكَفِّهِ لِلْعَيْنِ رَدْ

لِقَتَادَةٍ مِنْ فَوْقِ خَدْ

With his hand he restored the eye
of Qatāda, that hung down on his cheek

هَذَا النَّبِيُّ لَهُ مَدَدْ

خَيْرُ الأَنَامِ العَرَبِي

This Prophet possesses support
the best of mankind, the Arab

يَا سَعْدَ مَنْ زَارُوا الحَبِيبْ

فِي رَوْضَةٍ فِيهَا يَطِيبْ

How lucky are those who visit the Beloved
at the Rawḍa, there it becomes good

عَيْشُ المُسَافِرِ وَ القَرِيبْ

فَالْوَقْتُ وَقْتُ الطَّرَبِ

The livelihood of travellers and those nearby,
the time is one of delight

فَاطْرَبْ بِهِ يَا مَنْ أَحَبْ

لِنَبِيِّهِ وَ لَهُ أَقْتَرَبْ

So delight in him, O you who loves
your Prophet, and to him draw near

وَ الشُّكْرُ حَقًّا قَدْ وَجَبْ

عِنْدَ النَّبِيِّ العَرَبِي

Surely thankfulness is a duty
owed in the presence of the Arab Prophet

وَ انْظُرْ إِلَىٰ نُورِ الضَّرِيحْ

فِيهِ النَّبِيُّ هُوَ المَلِيحْ

Look at the light of the grave:
Therein is the Prophet, the pleasant one!

قَدْ فَاقَ آدَمَ وَ المَسِيحْ

خَيْرُ الأَنَامِ العَرَبِي

He excelled Adam and the Messiah
the best of mankind, the Arab

مَلْجَانَا ذُو الخُلُقِ العَظِيمْ

قَدْ فَاقَ نُوحاً وَ الكَلِيمْ

Our refuge, possessing an immense character
he surpassed Nūh and al-Kalīm[45]

45 Sayyiduna Mūsā ﷺ

ذُو رَأْفَةٍ وَ هُوَ الرَّحِيمْ
خَيْرُ الأَنَامِ العَرَبِي

Possessing compassion, he is merciful
the best of mankind, the Arab

وَ الخَلْقُ فِي يَوْمٍ عَظِيمْ
قَدْ أَقْبَلُوا نَحْوَ الرَّحِيمْ

Creation on the mighty Day
they will approach the merciful

نَالُوا الشَّفَاعَةَ مِنْ كَرِيمْ
خَيْرِ الأَنَامِ العَرَبِي

They will obtain intercession from one who is generous
the best of mankind, the Arab

وَ لِوَاؤُهُ فَوْقَ الجَمِيعْ
فَهُوَ المُشَفَّعُ وَ الشَّفِيعْ

His banner is above all
he is the intercessor whose intercession is accepted

لِلَّهِ يَا نِعْمَ المُطِيعْ
خَيْرُ الأَنَامِ العَرَبِي

What a good, obedient slave of Allah!
the best of mankind, the Arab

مَا مِثْلُهُ عَبْدٌ وَدُودْ

لِلَّهِ يُكْثِرُ لِلسُّجُودْ

Unparalleled, an affectionate slave
prostrating to Allah frequently

أَوْفَى الخَلَائِقِ بِالعُهُودْ

خَيْرُ الأَنَامِ العَرَبِي

The most faithful of creatures to covenants
the best of mankind, the Arab

مَمْدُوحٌ فِي سُوَرِ الكِتَابْ

وَ اللّهِ أَلْهَمَهُ الصَّوَابْ

Lauded in the chapters of the Book
Allah inspired properness to him

وَ عَنْ الدُّنَا رُفِعَ العَذَابْ

بِظُهُورِ خَيْرِ العَرَبِ

Punishment is lifted from the world
by the appearance of the best of Arabs

ذُو المُعْجِزَاتِ الثَّابِتَاتْ

البَيِّنَاتِ الوَاضِحَاتْ

Possessor of verified miracles,
clear and plain for all to see

تَبْقَى إِلَى بَعْدِ المَمَاتْ

خَيْرُ الأَنَامِ العَرَبِي

Enduring after death
the best of mankind, the Arab

أَحْيَاهُ رَبِّي بَعْدَمَا

ذَاقَ المَمَاتَ وَ أَكْرِما

My Lord gave him life after
he tasted death, ennobled

إِذْهَبْ إِلَيْهِ مُسَلِّمَا

تَلْقَاهُ خَيْرَ العَرَبِ

Go to him in a state of submission
you'll meet him, the best of Arabs

إِذْهَبْ إِلَيْهِ وَ لا تَخَفْ

تَلْقَ المَسَرَّةَ وَ التُّحَفْ

Go to him and do not fear
you will receive happiness and gifts

يَا سَعْدَ مَنْ يَوْماً وَقَفْ

عِنْدَ النَّبِيِّ العَرَبِي

How fortunate is the one who one day stands
in the presence of the Arab Prophet

نَادَاهُ يَا خَيْرَ الأَنَامْ

إِنِّي أَتَيْتُكَ بِالهُيَامْ

Who calls him, 'O best of mankind!
I have come to you madly in love

أَهْدِيكَ مِنْ قَلْبِي السَّلَامْ

وَ انْظُرْ وَرَاءَ الحُجُبِ

From my heart I extend you greetings
look from behind the veil'

وَ انْظُرْ بِقَلْبِكَ نُورَهُ

وَ انْشَقْ أُخَيَّ عُطُورَهُ

Look with your heart at his light
inhale, O my brother, his perfumes

وَ ادْخُلْ حِمَاهُ وَ سُورَهُ

تَلْقَاهُ خَيْرَ العَرَبِ

Enter his sanctuary and enclosure
you will meet him, the best of Arabs

أُنْظُرْ بِرُوحِكَ وَ اسْتَمِعْ

فَإِذَا رَأَيْتَ فَلَا تُذِعْ

Look with your soul and listen
and when you see, do not divulge

ثَبِّتْ فُؤَادَكَ وَ اقْتَنِعْ

هَذَا خِيَارُ العَرَبِ

Strengthen your heart, contented
this is the choicest of Arabs

وَقَفَ المُحِبُّ بِبَابِهِ

وَ لَجَا لِفَضْلِ جَنَابِهِ

The lover stands by his door,
taking refuge by virtue of his excellency,

مُتَشَرِّفاً بِرِحَابِهِ

خَيْرُ الأَنَامِ العَرَبِي

Honored by his magnanimity
the best of mankind, the Arab

نَظَرَ النَّبِيُّ لِمَنْ حَضَرْ

عِنْدَ المَقَامِ عَلَى قَدَرْ

The Prophet looks at him who is present
at the maqam, by a Decree

نَالَ الشَّفَاعَةَ وَ الوَطَرْ

عِنْدَ النَّبِيِّ الطَّيِّبِ

He obtains intercession and his desire
with the pure Prophet

جَاءُوا أُلُوفاً زَائِرِينْ
مِنْ كُلِّ فَجٍّ وَافِدِينْ

In thousands they come, visiting,
from every mountain pass, in delegations

وَصَلُوا إِلَى بَابِ الأَمِينْ
خَيْرِ الأَنَامِ العَرَبِي

They reach the door of the Trustworthy
the best of mankind, the Arab

فَرِحُوا بِهِ زَادَ السُّرُورْ
وَ اللهُ ضَاعَفَ لِلأُجُورْ

They rejoice over him and the happiness increases
and Allah multiplies the reward

نُورٌ لَهُ فَاقَ البُدُورْ
خَيْرُ الأَنَامِ العَرَبِي

His light surpasses full moons
the best of mankind, the Arab

رَدُّ السَّلَامَ عَلَيْهِمُ
بِبَشَاشَةٍ إِذْ سَلَّمُوا

He returns their greetings
with a smile when they salute

حَيَّاهُمُ لَبَّاهُمُ

خَيْرُ الأَنَامِ العَرَبِي

He greets them, responding to them
the best of mankind, the Arab

قَالُوا السَّلَامُ عَلَى العَتِيقْ

وَ صَدِيقِهِ نِعْمَ الصَّدِيقْ

They convey greetings to the noble one,
his friend[46]. What an excellent friend indeed!

فِي الغَارِ يَا نِعْمَ الرَّفِيقْ

لِلْهَاشِمِيِّ العَرَبِي

In the cave, what a excellent companion
for the Hāshimī Arab

قَالُوا السَّلَامُ عَلَى عُمَرْ

نِعْمَ الشَّهِيدُ لَهُ انْتَصَرْ

They convey greetings to ʿUmar
what an excellent martyr, triumphant!

بِجِوَارِهِ فِي الخُلْدِ قَرْ

عِنْدَ النَّبِي العَرَبِي

Established eternally beside him
in the presence of the Arab Prophet

46 Sayyidunā Abū Bakr ﵁

عُثْمَانُ مِنَّا لَكَ السَّلَامْ

يَا جَامِعاً خَيْرَ الكَلَامْ

Greetings from us to you, ʿUthmān
O gatherer of the fairest speech

فِي عُسْرَةٍ نِلْتَ المَرَامْ

عِنْدَ النَّبِيِّ العَرَبِي

In distress you obtained your wish
with the Arab Prophet

وَ لَكَ السَّلَامُ أَيَا عَلِي

يَا بَابَ عِلْمِ المُرْسَلِ

Greetings to you, ʿAlī,
O door to knowledge of the Envoy

أَنْتَ الوَصِيُّ كَذَا الْوَلِي

عِنْدَ النَّبِيِّ العَرَبِي

You are the trustee and the intimate friend as well
of the Arab Prophet

سَلِّمْ عَلَيْهِمْ كُلَّمَا

زُرْتَ النَّبِيِّ فَإِنَّمَا

Greet them whenever
you visit the Prophet. Indeed,

هُمْ بِالجِوَارِ وَ طَالَمَا
سَمِعُوا حَدِيثَ الطَّيِّبِ

They are nearby, and how often
they heard the speech of the Pure one

يَا رَبِّ صَلِّ مَعَ السَّلَامْ
لِلْمُصْطَفَى خَيْرِ الأَنَامِ

My Lord, send prayers with greetings
on the Chosen one, the best of humans,

وَ الآلِ وَ الصَّحْبِ الكِرَامْ
مَا فَاحَ فَيْحُ الطَّيِّبِ

And on the family and the noble companions
as long as the fragrance the pure one exudes,

مَا الجَعْفَرِي نَظَمَ الدُّرَرْ
فِي مَدْحِ مَنْ فَاقَ القَمَرْ

So long as al-Jaʿfarī arranges pearls
in praise of him who outshone the moon

يَرْجُو الشَّفَاعَةَ وَ النَّظَرْ
مِنْ هَاشِمِيٍّ طَيِّبِ

Hoping for intercession and a look
from the pure Hāshimī

إِغْفِرْ ذُنُوبِي يَا غَفُورْ
أُسْتُرْ عُيُوبِي يَا شَكُورْ

Forgive my sins, O All-Forgiving One!
Cover up my vices, O Appreciative One!

ضَاعِفْ بِفَضْلِكَ لِلأُجُورْ
بِالهَاشِمِيِّ الطَّيِّبِ

Magnify rewards by Your favor
by means of the pure Hāshimī

فَوَّضْتُ أَمْرِى إِلَىٰ الجَلِيلِ
اللّٰهُ حَسْبِي وَ الوَكِيلْ

I have entrusted my matter to the Majestic One
Allah is my sufficiency and Guardian

وَ دَخَلْتُ فِي جَاهِ الكَفِيلْ
خَيْرِ الأَنَامِ العَرَبِي

I entered the rank of the guarantor,
the best of mankind, the Arab

وَ جَعَلْتُ مَدْحِى سُلَّمَا
لِرِضَاهُ كَيْمَا أَسْلَمَا

I made my eulogy a ladder
to his pleasure to grant me safety

مِنْ كُلِّ شَرٍّ بَعْدَمَا

أَحْبَبْتُ خَيْرَ العَرَبِ

From every evil after
loving the best of Arabs

وَ بِنُورِهِ خُتِمَ الكَلَامْ

وَ بِجَاهِهِ نِلْتُ المَرَامْ

By his light the speech was sealed
and by his glorious rank I attained my wish

إِنْ شَاءَ رَبِّي لَا أُلَامْ

عِنْدَ النَّبِيِّ العَرَبِي

If my Lord wills I will not be hurt
in the presence of the Arab Prophet

يَا مَنْ يُرِيدُ نَجَاتَهُ

إِلزَمْ عَلَيْكَ صَلاَتَهُ

O you wishing for salvation
persist in sending prayers on him!

إِجْلِبْ بِهَا مَرْضَاتَهُ

خَيْرُ الأَنَامِ العَرَبِي

Draw from them his pleasure
the best of mankind, the Arab

فَهِيَ النَّجَاةُ المُسْرِعَةْ

فِيهَا الكُنُوزُ المُودَعَهْ

That is the expedited rescue
containing the stored treasures

خَيْرُ الوَرَى مَا أَنْفَعَهْ

خَيْرُ الأَنَامِ العَرَبِي

The best of creatures, how beneficial!
The best of mankind, the Arab

إِنْ ضَاقَ صَدْرُكَ بِالكَدَرْ

عَرِّجْ عَلَى خَيْرِ البَشَرْ

If your heart is constricted by turbidity,
turn to the choicest of humans

فَهُوَ الشَّفِيعُ المُنْتَظَرْ

خَيْرُ الأَنَامِ العَرَبِي

He is the anticipated intercessor
the best of mankind, the Arab

-12-

# Everyone Withdrew

وَ صَلاةٌ وَ سَلامٌ

لِنَبِيٍّ جَاءَ يُنْبِي

Prayers of blessings and greetings of peace
on a Prophet who came informing

غَابَ كُلٍّ غَابَ قَلْبِي

عَنْ سِوَى مَوْلَاىَ رَبِّي

Everyone withdrew! My heart withdrew
from other than my Master, my Lord

مَا عَذَابِي فِي حَيَاتِي

غَيْرُ بُعْدِى غَيْرُ حَجْبِي

My only punishment in this life
is my distance, my veil

يَا أُهَيْلَ الْوُدِّ هَيَّا
فَاسْمَحُوا يَوْمًا بِقُرْبِي

O devotees of love, come!
Allow me one day to draw closer

إِنَّنِي عَبْدٌ ذَلِيلٌ
خَائِفٌ مِنْ هَوْلِ ذَنْبِي

I am a lowly slave,
afraid of the horror of my sinfulness

وَ رَجَائِي وَ اعْتِمَادِي
مَحْضُ فَضْلِ اللَّهِ رَبِّي

My hope and my reliance
are a pure favor of Allah, my Lord

أَرْتَجِي الرَّحْمٰنَ رَبِّي
نَظْرَةً تُحْيِي لِقَلْبِي

I hope from the All-Merciful, my Lord
for a look that enlivens my heart

وَ مُرَادِي وَ مُنَائِي
زَوْرَةُ الْمُخْتَارِ حِبِّي

My intention and my desire
is visiting the Chosen one, my love

لَا أُبَالِي بِاغْتِرَابِي
إِذْ رَأَيْتُ اللّٰهَ حَسْبِي

I am unbothered by my estrangement
since I realize Allah is my sufficiency

كُنْ نَصِيرِي يَا إِلَٰهِي
وَ انْصُرَنْ أَهْلِي وَ حِزْبِي

Be my supporter, O God
and assist my family and my party

كُلَّمَا فَكَّرْتُ يَوْمًا
فِي أُمُوْرِي قَالَ لُبِّي

Whenever one day I pondered
over my affairs, my core declared

جَرِّدِ النَفْسَ لِرَبِّ
نَحْوَ بَيْتِ اللّٰهِ لَبِّي

Devote yourself to the Lord
go towards the House of Allah, chanting *Labbayk*!

لا تُفَكِّرْ فِي أُمُوْرٍ
لَسْتَ تَدْرِي عِلْمَ غَيْبِ

Do not speculate on matters
as you do not comprehend the knowledge of the unseen

وَ اذْكُرِ اللّٰهَ تَعَالَى

وَ احْفَظِ الشَّيْخَ المُرَبِّي

Rather, remember Allah, the Exalted
and take hold to the mentoring guide

إِنَّمَا الشَّيْخُ إِمَامٌ

بِعُيُوبِ النَفْسِ يُنْبِ

The guide is indeed an Imām[47]
apprising one of the ailments of the self

طَاعَةُ الشَّيْخِ أَمَانٌ

مِنْ خَيَالاتٍ وَ سَلْبِ

Obedience to the guide is safety
from false imaginings and deprivation

مَنْ أَتَى مِنْ غَيْرِ شَيْخِ

ضَلَّ فِي مَيْدَانِ حَرْبِ

Whoever comes without a guide
gets lost on the battlefield

فَالْزَمِ البَابَ وَ جَاهِدْ

وَ ادْخُلَنْ فِي جَمْعِ سِرْبِ

Cling to the door and strive
and join a gathering of hearts

47 Leader or authority.

تَلْقَ سُهَّارَ اللَّيَالِي
بِصَلاةٍ أَوْ بِجَذْبِ

You will meet the devotees of night vigil
engaged in prayer, Divinely pulled

عَمَرُوا الكَوْنَ فَكَانُوا
كَبُدُورٍ بَيْنَ صَحْبِ

They populate the Cosmos, becoming
like full moons amid companions

أَحْمَدُ بْنُ ادْرِيسَ شَيْخِي
وَارِثُ المُخْتَارِ حِبِّي

Aḥmad b. Idrīs, my guide,
heir to the Chosen one, my love

مِنْ يَدَيْهِ العِلْمُ يُتْلَى
لا بِكُرَّاسٍ وَ كُتْبِ

In front of him, knowledge is recited
without notebooks or writings

قَالَ خَتْمُ الْقَوْمِ فِيهِ
إِنَّهُ نِعْمَ المُرَبِّي

About him the seal of the People said,
'What a wonderful nurturer he is!'

يَقْرَأُ القُرْآنَ لَيْلاً

خَاتِماً قُرْآنَ رَبِّي

He recites the Qur'ān at night
completing the whole Qur'ān of my Lord

رَكْعَةٌ أُوْلَى وَ أُخْرَى

تَمَّ شَيْخِي كُلَّ حِزْبِ

One rak'ah after another
my guide completes every *ḥizb*

لَسْتُ أَدْرِي مِثْلَ شَيْخِي

مِنْ شُيُوْخِ الكَوْنِ حَسْبِي

I know no one like my guide
from the guides all over the world [he is] my sufficiency

وَ صَلاةٌ وَ سَلاَمٌ

لِنَبِيٍّ جَاءَ يُبْنِي

Prayers of blessings and greetings of peace
on a Prophet who came informing

ثُمَّ آلِ البَيْتِ طُرًّا

وَ أُحَيْبَابٍ وَ صَحْبِ

Then on all family members without exception,
loved ones and Companions

مَا تَغَنَّى بِمَدِيحٍ
صَالِحٌ يَرْجُو لِقُرْبِ

So long as Ṣāliḥ seeking nearness
chants some words of eulogy

وَ خِتَاماً يَا إِلَهِي
لا تُزِغْ يَوْما لِقَلْبِي

Lastly, O my God
do not let my heart stray even for a day

وَ اطْرُدِ الأَعْدَاءَ طَرْداً
أَنْتَ يَا أللّهُ حَسْبِي

And chase the enemies away forcefully
You, O Allah, are my sufficiency!

## -13-

## A Pleasant Time

يَا رَبِّ صَلِّ عَلَى النَّبِيِّ وَ آلِهِ
وَ تَعَمُّ مَنْ كَانُوا لَهُ أَصْحَابَا

Lord, send prayers on the Prophet and on his family
including all those who were to him companions

طَابَ الزَّمَانُ بِكُمْ بِخَيْرٍ طَابَا
لَمَّا رَأَتْكُمْ مُهْجَتِي أَحْبَابَا

Time with you is delightful in good
when my soul sees you as beloved

وَ تَعَطَّرَتْ أَيَّامُنَا بِوِدَادِكُمْ
مِنْ فَرْطِ حُبِّكُمُ الكَبِيرُ تَصَابَى

Our days are perfumed by your love
intense love for you turns the adult childlike

وَ وِدَادُكُمْ مَا غَابَ عَنْ أَرْوَاحِنَا
كَلَّا بِجَاهِ مُحَمَّدٍ مَا غَابَا

Your love is not hidden from our spirits
no, by the glory of Muḥammad it is not absent!

وَ العَارِفُونَ بِكُمْ لَدَيْهِمْ نَشْوَةٌ
أَحْيَتْ قُلُوبَهُمْ كَصَيْبٍ صَابَا

Those cognizant of you are gripped by intoxication
enlivening their hearts as if rain falling heavily

وَ الزَّائِرُونَ لَكُمْ لَدَيْهِمْ حَضْرَةٌ
حَضَرُوا بِهَا وَ تَبَادَلُوا الأَكْوَابَا

Those visiting you have a presence
by which they attend, exchanging goblets

شَرِبُوا رَحِيقَ الحُبِّ مِنْ بَحْرِ الصَّفَا
فَتَحُوا لَهُمْ مِنْ حُبِّكُمْ أَبْوَابَا

They drink the nectar of love from the sea of purity
they opened for them doors out of their love for you

وَ جُلُوسُهُمْ فِي دَارِكُمْ يَا سَادَتِي
نَالُوا بِهِ التَّقْوَى فَكُلٌّ تَابَا

By sitting in your house, O my masters
they gain taqwā, so everyone repents

التَّائِبُونَ العَابِدُونَ بِدَارِكُمْ
لَبِسُوا التُّقَى يَا سَادَتِي أَثْوَابَا

The worshipping penitents at your residence
wear taqwā as their dress, O my masters!

وَ الوَاقِفُونَ بِبَابِكُمْ يَا سَادَتِي
كُلٌّ يَنَالُ مِنَ الجَزَاءِ ثَوَابَا

Those standing by your door, O my masters
each one is receiving as recompense a great reward

قَدْ أَشْبَهُوا الأَمْلَاكَ فِي وَقَفَاتِهِمْ
كَالوَاقِفِينَ بِرَوْضَةٍ أَحبَابَا

They resemble angels in their standing
like those standing at the Rawḍa as lovers

نَظَرُوا المَقَامَ لَدَيْكُمُ فَتَذَكَّرُوا
ذَاكَ المَقَامَ فَرَحَّبُوا تَرْحَابَا

At your maqam they look and remember
that maqam, and welcome you with a greeting

سَكَبُوا دُمُوعَ الحُبِّ لَمَّا شَاهَدُوا
مِنْكُمْ مَقَاماً مُشْبِهاً مَا غَابَا

Tears of love they shed when they witness
a maqam of yours resembling what was distant

ذَاكَ الْمَقَامُ بِطَيْبَةٍ فِيهِ الَّذِى
مَلَأَ الْوُجُودَ مَكَارِماً وَ صَوَابَا

That maqam in Ṭāyba hosting the one
who filled existence with noble deeds and properness

تَلْقَاهُ بَسَّاماً بِوَجْهٍ مُشْرِقٍ
وَ لَدَيْهِ عِلْمٌ أَعْجَزَ الْكُتَّابَا

You meet him smiling with a radiant face,
regaled with a knowledge which incapacitates the scribes

مِنْ فَضْلِ رَبِّى لَا بِقَوْلِ مُعَلِّمٍ
سُبْحَانَ مَنْ أَعْطَى النَّبِيَّ كِتَابَا

Out of my Lord's favor, not a speech by a teacher,
glory to the One Who gave the Prophet a Book

جَمَعَ الْعُلُومَ جَمِيعَهَا فِى آيِهِ
قَدْ حَذَّرَ الْخَلْقَ الْجَمِيعَ حِسَابَا

Gathering all sciences in one Sign
warning the whole creation of a Reckoning

وَ دَعَاهُمْ لِعِبَادَةِ الرَّبِّ الَّذِى
خَلَقَ الْأَنَامَ وَ سَبَّبَ الْأَسْبَابَا

It calls them to worship of the Lord Who
created humans, and produced the means of subsistence

يَا رَوْضَةً فِيهَا النَّبِيُّ مُحَمَّدٌ

سَمِعَ النِّدَاءِ لِزَائِرٍ فَأَجَابَا

O Rawḍa hosting the Prophet Muḥammad
who heard the call of the visitor and answered

يَا مَرْحَباً بِأَحِبَّةٍ جَاءُوا لَهَا

يَجْزِيهِمُ الرَبُّ الكَرِيمُ ثَوَابَا

Welcome to lovers that have come
the Generous Lord will repay them with bounties

يَا أَيُّهَا النَّاسُ الكِرَامُ تَقَدَّمُوا

نَحْوَ المَدِينَةِ قَاصِدِينَ لِطَابَا

O noble people, advance
towards Madīna, in the direction of Ṭābā

لِيَطِيبَ وَقْتُكُمْ بِطِيبِ رِيَاضِهَا

وَ تَرَوْنَ ذَا كَرَمٍ يَفُوقُ سَحَابَا

For your time to be pleasant in its pleasant meadows
looking at a generous one surpassing the clouds,

وَ تَرَوْنَ ذَا نُورٍ يَفُوقُ بِنُورِهِ

شَمْسَ الزَّمَانِ وَ يُكْرِمُ الأَصْحَابَا

Looking at an illumined one whose light has excelled
the sun of the time, and companions he honors

ذَاكَ النَّبِيُّ مُحَمَّدٌ أَكْرِمْ بِهِ
أَحْيَ اللَّيَالِي دَايِماً أَوَّابَا

That is Prophet Muḥammad, so honor him
he enlivened the nights incessantly repentant

وَ تَوَرَّمَتْ قَدَمَاهُ لَمَّا شَاقَهُ
طُولُ القِيَامِ وَ دَمْعُهُ سَكَّابَا

His feet were swollen when weighed down
by lengthy standing, as his tears rolled down

مَنْ مِثْلُهُ فِي الكَوْنِ يَذْكُرُ رَبَّهُ
سَبَقَ الأَوَائِلَ لَمْ يَكُنْ هَيَّابَا

Who is like him in the Universe remembering his Lord?
The early ones he outstripped, he was not timorous

يَا شَاغِلَ اللَّيلِ الطَّوِيلِ بِنَوْمِهِ
إِخْشَ المَلَامَةَ مِنْهُ وَ اخْشَ عِتَابَا

O you filling the long night by your sleep,
beware of reproach from him, and beware of reproof

فَمَتَى القِيَامُ وَ أَنْتَ تَطْلُبُ فَانِياً
مَشْغُولَ قَلْبٍ لَمْ تَكُنْ تَوَّابَا

When will you stand up, while searching for the transient,
engrossing a heart that eschews repentance?

سَهَرُ اللَّيَالِي لِلرِّجَالِ كَمَعْشَرٍ
شَنُّوا الإِغَارَةَ شَتَّتُوا الأَحْزَابَا

Keeping vigil at night is for men like a troop
launching an attack and splitting the bands

إِنْ كُنْتَ ذَا سَيْفٍ فَجَرِّدْ مُرْهَفاً
وَ اضْرِبْ لِأَعْدَاءٍ وَ كُنْ ضَرَّابَا

If you are a swordsman, unsheathe a sharpened tool,
and strike the enemies, and be vehement against

شَيْطَانَ نَفْسِكَ وَ الهَوَى وَ مَعَارِفاً
أَخَذُوكَ نَحْوَ الذُّلِّ كُنْ هَرَّابَا

the devil, your ego, passion and notions
carrying you to abasement, and flee then to safety!

مَنْ لَمْ يَقُمْ بِاللَّيْلِ أَفْلَسَ نَفْسَهُ
فَإِذَا رَأَيْتَ رَأَيْتَ ثُمَّ سَرَابَا

Whoever shuns night worship, bankrupts his nafs
if you look at him, you see nothing but a mirage

هَيْهَاتَ هَيْهَاتَ العَتِيقُ لِمَعْشَرٍ
جَعَلُوا الوِلَايَةَ أَنْ تُرَى وَثَّابَا

How preposterous, the ancient traditions of this assembly
turn sainthood to being seen jumping around

لِحُطَامِ دُنْيَاهُمْ وَ تِلْكَ مُصِيبَةٌ
كَانَ الحُطَامُ بِأَهْلِهِ ذَهَّابَا

For the rubble of their dunya, truly a calamity!
Rubble is fleeting with its people

يَا مَيِّتَا تَرَكَ الحُطَامَ وَ دَارَه
هَلَّا اتَّخَذْتَ لِمِثْلِ ذَا جِلْبَابَا

O dead man who discarded debris and his home,
should you not adopt the like of this as a garment?

عُرْيَانَ تَخْرُجُ مِنْ دِيَارِكَ حَافِياً
وَ تَرَكْتَ دُنْيَا وَ افْتَرَشْتَ تُرَابَا

You exit your home naked, barefoot
you left the lower world and lied down on the ground

هَلْ بَعْدَ ذَلِكَ تَسْتَطِيعُ عِبَادَةْ
وَ تَقُومُ لَيْلاً أَوْ تَقُولُ كِتَابَا

Can you engage after that in worship
keeping vigil at night and reciting the Book?

هَيِّءْ لِدَارِكَ قَبْلَ مَوْتِكَ إِنَّهَا
دَارُ الخُلُودِ وَ لَا تَكُنْ سَخَّابَا

Prepare for your abode before you die, as it is
an everlasting abode, and do not be one unlearned

وَ افْرَحْ بِرَبِّكَ وَ اذْكُرَنَّ جَلَالَهُ
تَلْقَ المُهَيْمِنَ دَايِماً وَهَّابَا

Rejoice at your Lord, and mention His Majesty:
you will meet the Guardian, incessantly bestowing

وَ افْرَحْ بِهِ فَرَحاً عَظِيماً يَا فَتَى
فَإِذَا فَرِحْتَ فَلَا تَكُنْ مُرْتَابَا

Rejoice at Him boundlessly, O young man
and if you then rejoice, do not be skeptical

جَاءَ الكِتَابُ بِهَذِهِ فِي آيَةٍ
أُتْلُ الكِتَابَ تَجِدْ هُنَاكَ صَوَابَا

The Book brought these truths in a Sign
recite the Book, you will find there correctness

فَإِذَا فَرِحْتَ بِهِ فَتِلْكَ عَطِيَّةٌ
مَا مِثْلُهَا شَيْءٌ لِمَنْ هُوَ غَابَا

If you rejoice at it, that is a gift
there is nothing like it for the one withdrawn

عَنْ هَذِهِ الدُّنْيَا وَ عَنْ لِذَّاتِهَا
وَ رَأَى الجِنَانَ نَعِيمَهَا سَكَّابَا

From this world and its passions
who sees bliss pouring forth, in Gardens

فَاتْلُ الكِتَابَ بِلَيلِهِ مُتَهَجِّداً
هَذَا السَّبِيلُ فَكُنْ لَهُ مُنْسَابَا

Recite then the Book, keeping vigil at night
this is the path, so hasten to it

فَإذَا تَرَكْتَ فَمَا وَصَلْتَ فَلَا تَكُنْ
عَبْدَ المَنَامِ وَ كُنْ لَهُ رَهَّابَا

If you abandon it, you will not arrive. So do not be
a slave to sleep, but be to it an ascetic

وَ اسْجُدْ لَهُ لَيْلاً طَوِيلاً إِنْ تَكُنْ
أَحْيَيْتَ لَيْلاً لَا تَكُنْ عَطَّابَا

Prostrate to Him at length at night if you
enliven the night, you will not be fatigued

وَ دَخَلْتَ فِي كَنَفِ الإِلَهِ وَ حِصْنِهِ
أُعْطِيْتَ نُوراً قَدْ كَشَفْتَ حِجَابَا

You will enter God's fortress, under His protection
you will be gifted a light, removing a veil

وَ نَظَرْتَ مَا نَظَرَ الأَوَائِلُ فِي الدُّجَى
وَ رَآكَ رَبُّكَ قَانِتاً تَوَّابَا

You will see what the early ones saw in darkness
and your Lord will see you devout and repentant

ثُمَّ الصَّلَاةُ عَلَى النَّبِيِّ وَ آلِهِ
وَ تَعُمُّ مَنْ كَانُوا لَهُ أَصْحَابَا

Then prayers on the Prophet and on his family
including all those who were to him companions

وَ كَذَا السَّلَامُ بِقَدْرِ مَا صَلَّى الأَوْلَى
غَيْثاً يَعُمُّ مَنَازِلاً وَ قِبَابَا

And greeting, commensurate to what the elite have prayed
pouring down as rain extending to houses and tents

مَا الجَعْفَرِيُّ يَقُولُ فِي مَدْحِ الَّذِى
لَوْلَاهُ مَا قَرَأَ الأَنَامُ كِتَابَا

So long as al-Jaʿfarī eulogizes the one
if not for him, no one would have read the Book

لَوْلَاهُ مَا كَانَ الحَجِيجُ بِمَكَّةٍ
لَوْلَاهُ مَا ذَهَبَ الأَنَامُ لِطَابَا

If not for him, no pilgrim would be found in Makka,
if not for him, no person would ever go to Ṭābā.

## -14-

## Zaynab

أَزَيْنَبُ أَنْتِ فِي الدُّنْيَا كَشَمْسٍ
لَهَا نُورٌ يُضِيءُ وَ لَا تَغِيبُ

Zaynab, you are in this world like a sun
whose light illumines and never sets

وَ مَنْ جَاءَ المَقَامَ إِلَيْكِ يُشْفَى
بِإِذْنِ اللَّهِ أَنْتِ لَهُ الطَّبِيبُ

Whoever comes to you by the maqam is healed
by Allah's leave, you are for him the doctor

وَ مِنْ بَرَكَاتِ جَدِّكِ كُنْتِ ذُخْراً
وَ قَلْبُ الزَّائِرِينَ هُنَا يَطِيبُ

From the blessing of your Grandfather, you are preserved,
here the hearts of the visitors find rehabilitation

يُشَفِّعُكِ الإِلَهُ لِكُلِّ عَبْدٍ
يَزُورُكِ مُخْلِصاً وَ لَهُ نَحِيبُ

The Divine grants you intercession for every slave
who visits you sincerely, sobbing

وَ هَا أَنَا قَدْ أَتَيْتُ إِلَيْكِ أَسْعَى
غَرِيبٌ فِي البِلَادِ وَ مَا غَرِيبُ

Here I am: to you I have hastened
a stranger in the country, and yet no stranger

وَ مَنْ وَصَلَ المَقَامَ رَآكِ أَهْلاً
أَباً أُمًّا وَ عَطْفُكِ ذَا عَجِيبُ

Whoever reaches the maqam sees you as family:
father, mother, and your sympathy is wondrous

وَ أَكْرَمَكِ الإِلَهُ بِكُلِّ خَيْرٍ
وَ مَنْ دَخَلَ المَقَامَ لَهُ نَصِيبُ

The Divine honored you with every good
he who enters the maqam will have a share

بِجَاهِ المُصْطَفَى خَيْرِ البَرَايَا
يَجِيءُ الخَيْرُ وَ الفَتْحُ القَرِيبُ

By the status of the Chosen one, the best of creatures
goodness and an impending opening comes

سَأَلْتُ اللّٰهَ يَمْنَحُنِي بِعَفْوٍ
فَيَا نِعْمَ الإِلٰهُ هُوَ المُجِيبُ

I asked Allah to gift me a pardon
how excellent is the Divine! He is the Answerer

وَ أَصْحَابِي وَ إِخْوَانِي جَمِيعاً
بِجَاهِكِ لَا نَضِلُّ وَ لَا نَعِيبُ

My companions and brethren, all of them
by your rank we will not stray or be blemished

## -15-

## Lord, By My Love

صَلَّى عَلَيْكَ اللّٰهُ يَا خَيْرَ الوَرَى
يَا كَامِلَ الأَوْصَافِ ثُمَّ الذَّاتِ

Allah sends prayers on you, O best of creation
O one endowed with perfect attributes, and essence, too

رَبِّي بِحُبِّي لِلنَّبِيِّ وَ آلِهِ
أَبْدِلْ هَوَايَ بِصَالِحِ النِّيَّاتِ

My Lord, by my love for the Prophet and for his family,
replace my lust with wholesome intentions

وَ امْنُنْ عَلَيَّ بِرَحْمَةٍ وَ مَوَدَّةٍ
حَتَّى أَكُونَ مُيَسَّرَ الحَسَنَاتِ

Grace me with mercy and affection
that good actions might come easily to me

إِنِّي إِلَيْكَ بِأَحْمَدٍ مُتَوَجِّهٌ

خَيْرُ الأَنَامِ مُبَارَكُ الرَّوْضَاتِ

Indeed, I am turning to You by Aḥmad,
the best of creation, by meadows blessed

يَا خَيْرَ خَلْقِ اللّهِ إِنِّي سَابِلٌ

رَبِّي بِجَاهِكَ كَثْرَةَ الزَّوْرَاتِ

O best of Allah's creation, I am asking
my Lord, by your rank, for plentiful visits

وَ أَرَى مَقَامَكَ مُشْرِقاً وَ مُنَوِّراً

يُجْلَى بِهِ قَلْبِي مِنَ الزَّلَّاتِ

I see your maqam radiant and illumined
by it, slips are expunged from my heart

فَلِأَنْتَ نُورُ الكَوْنِ مِنْ ظُلِمَاتِهِ

يَا شَافِعٌ فِي الحَشْرِ فِي الكُرُبَاتِ

You are the light of existence bringing it out from darkness
O intercessor for those resurrected in distress!

الغَيْثُ يَنْزِلُ إِنْ دَعَوْتَ وَ هَكَذَا

يَرْضَاكَ رَبِّي قَابِلُ الدَّعَوَاتِ

Rain falls when you petition and thus
my Lord, Answerer of supplications, is pleased with you

كَمْ مِنْ أُمُورٍ قَدْ تَعَسَّرَ حَلُّهَا
لَكِنْ بِجَاهِكَ نِلْتُ لِلخَيْرَاتِ

How many a matter whose solution proved difficult,
yet by your status I obtain goodness

مَا خَابَ مَنْ قَصَدَ النَّبِيَّ مُحَمَّداً
وَ أَتَاهُ يَسْعَى فِي دُجَى الظُّلُمَاتِ

No one went wrong heading for the Prophet Muḥammad
hastening to him in the gloomy darkness

وَ رَأَى مَقَاماً فِيهِ خُلْدٌ طِيبُهُ
مِسْكٌ يَفُوحُ لِقَاصِدِ البَرَكَاتِ

He sees the maqam, in it is eternity, while his fragrance
of musk exudes to the seeker of blessings

كَمْ مِنْ مُحِبٍّ قَدْ تَهَلَّلَ وَجْهُهُ
لَمَّا رَآكَ مُبَارَكَ الجَلَسَاتِ

How many a lover whose face beamed joyfully
when he sighted the blessed gatherings

كَالبَدْرِ بَلْ كَالشَّمْسِ تَفْرَحُ عِنْدَمَا
جَاءُوا إِلَيْكَ أَحِبَّةُ الصَّلَوَاتِ

Like the full moon, nay, like the sun, you rejoice when
lovers of the prayer upon you approach

لَا سِيَّمَا قَوْمٌ رَأَيْتُ وُجُوهَهُمْ
تُضْوِى مِنَ السُّودَانِ فِي الحَلَقَاتِ

Especially people whose faces I saw
gleaming from Sudan in circles of worship

وَ الكُلُّ يَفْرَحُ بِالنَّبِيِّ وَ صَحْبِهِ
وَ يَرَوْنَ أُنْسَ الرُّوحِ فِي الجَنَّاتِ

They all rejoice at the Prophet and his Companions
watching the spirit's intimacy in the Gardens

لَوْلَاكَ يَا خَيْرَ الخَلَايِقِ كُلِّهِمْ
مَا كَانَ وَفْدٌ مِنْ بَعِيدٍ آتِي

Were it not for you, O best of all creatures,
no delegation would set out from afar

لَوْلَاكَ مَا قَطَعُوا الفِيَافِي ضَحْوَةً
وَ يَرَوْنَ ذَلِكَ أَفْضَلَ القُرُبَاتِ

Were it not for you, no desert would be crossed in mornings
yet they perceive that as the best source of nearness

أَنْتَ الحَبِيبُ وَ مَنْ أَحَبَّكَ قَدْ نَجَا
يَا رَبِّ بِالمُخْتَارِ أَرْجُو نَجَاتِي

You are the Beloved and whoever loves you is saved
O Lord, by the Chosen one I hope for my rescue

يَا صَاحِبَ الوَحْيِ الَّذِى مَا نَالَهُ
أَحَدٌ سِوَاهُ مُبَارَكَ الآيَاتِ

O recipient of Revelation which no one
but you attained the blessed āyāt

قَافٌ وَ نُونٌ وَ المَثَانِى كُلُّهَا
حِكَمٌ تُضِيءُ بِسَائِرِ البَلْدَاتِ

Qāf, Nūn, and all the oft-recited āyāt
wise pearls shining upon all lands

لَوْلَاكَ مَا سَمِعَ المَلَائِكَ هَذِهِ
كَلَّا وَ لَا قُرِئَتْ بِكُلِّ جِهَاتِ

Were it not for you, the angels would not hear them
no way, and they would not be read everywhere

كَالْغَيْثِ يَبْعَثُ فِى القُلُوبِ حَيَاتَهَا
تَحْيَا بِهِ مِنْ بَعْدِ طُولِ مَمَاتِ

Like the rain arousing life in the hearts
revived by it after a prolonged death

يَا صَاحِبَ السَّيْفِ الَّذِى رُفِعَتْ بِهِ
رَايَاتُ دِينِكَ صَاحِبَ الرَّايَاتِ

O wielder of the sword by which were lifted
the flags of your Dīn, O you with banners gifted

مَنْ مِثْلُ أَحْمَدَ فِي الْوُجُودِ لَهُ الْعُلَا
وَ رَقَى الطِّبَاقَ لِخَالِقِ الذَّرَّاتِ

Who in existence compares with Aḥmad, the lofty
he ascended the Heavens to the Creator of atoms

وَ رَأَى الْجَلِيلَ بِلَا مَثِيلٍ مُنَزَّهاً
عَنْ كُلِّ شَيْءٍ جَلَّ ذُو الدَّرَجَاتِ

He saw the Majestic, Incomparable, Transcendent
over everything, Exalted, Possessor of ranks

وَ أَتَى بِخَمْسٍ لِلْعِبَادِ ضِيَاؤُهَا
يُنْجِى بِيَوْمِ الْحَشْرِ ذِى الْحَسَرَاتِ

He brought five[48] to the slaves, their light
saves on the Day of Assembly, full of distress

يَا سَعْدَ مَنْ لَزِمَ الصَّلَاةَ فَإِنَّهُ
قَدْ جَاءَهُ الْمِعْرَاجُ بِالْبَرَكَاتِ

O fortunate one who clings to the prayer, indeed
the ascension brought him blessings

اللَّهُ بِالْمِعْرَاجِ أَعْلَى قَدْرَهُ
أَهْدَاهُ لِلْأَتْبَاعِ خَيْرَ هِبَاتِ

Allah by the ascension elevated his worth
gifting it to followers, the best of presents

---

48  The five daily prayers.

تِلْكَ الصَّلَاةُ هِيَ العِمَادُ فَلُذْ بِهَا
إِنْ صُنْتَهَا صَانَتْكَ مِنْ عَثَرَاتِ

That prayer is the support, so take shelter in it
if you guard it, it will guard you from errors

فَهِيَ الوِقَايَةُ وَ السَّلَامَةُ وَ الهُدَى
جَمَعَتْ لِكُلِّ الخَيْرِ فِي الرَّكَعَاتِ

It is protection, safety and guidance,
gathering every good in its units

لَوْلَاكَ مَا عَرَفَ الأَنَامُ صَلَاتَهُمْ
كَلَّا وَ لَا سَارُوا إِلَى عَرَفَاتِ

Were it not for you, humans would not have recognized their prayers
no indeed! And they would have not marched to ʾArafāt

كَلَّا وَ لَا جَاءُوا العَتِيقَ بِمَكَّةِ
لِطَوَافِ هَذَا البَيْتِ بِالدَّعَوَاتِ

No doubt, nor would they have come to the Ancient House in Makka
to make ṭawāf of this House supplicating

لَوْلَاكَ مَا رُفِعَتْ مَسَاجِدُ لِلتُّقَى
كَلَّا وَ لَا عَمَرَتْ مِنَ الصَّلَوَاتِ

Were it not for you, no masjid would have been built for taqwā
no way, nor would it be filled with any prayer

لَوْلَاكَ مَا شَدَّ الحَجِيجُ رِحَالَهُمْ

مُتَشَوِّقِينَ لِسَيِّدِ السَّادَاتِ

Were it not for you, no pilgrim would have saddled his mount
longing for the master of masters

صَلَّى عَلَيْكَ اللّٰهُ يَا خَيْرَ الوَرَى

يَا تَالِيَ القُرْآنِ فِي الأَوْقَاتِ

Allah sends prayers on you, O best of creation!
O reciter of the Qur'ān at all times

وَ الآلِ وَ الأَصْحَابِ مَا رَكْبٌ سَرَى

نَحْوَ النَّبِيِّ عَلَى أَتَمِّ صِفَاتِ

And on the family and the companions as long as the caravan travels
towards the Prophet in the manner most perfect

مَا الجَعْفَرِيُّ يَقُولُ فِي دَعَوَاتِهِ

أَبْدِلْ هَوَايَ بِصَالِحِ النِّيَّاتِ

So long as Ja'farī in his entreaties say,
'Replace my lust with wholesome intentions

وَفِّقْ لِأَصْحَابِي لِخَيْرِ مَسِيرِهِمْ

وَ احْفَظْهُمُ فِي سَائِرِ اللَحَظَاتِ

Grant to my companions the best of travels
and guard them in every moment'

وَ الجَعْفَرِيُّ هُوَ الشَّرِيفُ وَ جَدُّنَا
اِجْعَلْهُ يَا مَوْلَاىَ فِي الجَنَّاتِ

al-Ja'farī, he is noble [by lineage] and our grandfather
O my Master, place him in the Gardens

وَ بَنِيهِ وَ الأَهْلَ الكِرَامَ بِجَمْعِهِمْ
مِنْ آلِ جَعْفَرِ أَطْيَبِ الدَّوْحَاتِ

With his offspring, his noble household in full,
descendants of Ja'far, the purest family tree

لِأُهُمِ إِنِّى جَعْفَرِيٌّ نِسْبَةً
وَافَقْ لِقَوْلِى سَيِّدُ السَّادَاتِ

Considering that I am Ja'farī by lineage
the master of masters has agreed with my speech

هَذَا بِفَضْلِ اللَّهِ جَلَّ جَلَالَهُ
فَلَهُ الثَّنَاءُ عَلَى مَدَى الحَالَاتِ

This by favor of Allah, Majestically Extolled
to Him belongs the praise, state after state

## -16-

## Lord, By the Chosen One

يَا رَبِّ صَلِّ عَلَى المُخْتَارِ سَيِّدِنَا
مَنْ جَاءَ يَهْدِى الوَرَى أَنْوَارَ حِكْمَتِهِ

Lord, send prayers on the Chosen one, our master
who came guiding creatures to the lights of his wisdom

يَا رَبِّ بِالمُصْطَفَى طَهَ تُبَلِّغُهُ
مِنِّي السَّلَامَ وَ أَسْعِدْنِي بِرُؤْيَتِهِ

O Lord, by the Chosen one, Ṭāhā, convey to him
my greeting, and by his vision make me happy

مَتَى أُشَاهِدُ لِلأَنْوَارِ سَاطِعَةً
كَالشَّمْسِ تَظْهَرُ فِي أَرْكَانِ قُبَتِهِ

When I witness the radiant lights appearing,
like the sun on the pillars of his dome

مَتَى أُشَاهِدُ قَبْراً فِيهِ رَحْمَتُنَا

فِيهِ الَّذِى نَارَتِ الدُّنْيَا بِمِلَّتِهِ

When I witness a grave wherein our mercy lies,
wherein is the one who enlightened the world with his faith

مُحَمَّدٌ أَحْمَدٌ طَهَ الَّذِى نَزَلَتْ

مَلَائِكُ اللَّهِ تَأْيِيداً لِنُصْرَتِهِ

Muḥammad, Aḥmad, ṬāHā, for whom, the angels
of Allah, descended in support of his triumph

هَذَا الشَّفِيعُ لِفَصْلٍ فِى القَضَاءِ إِذَا

تَحَيَّرَ الكُلُّ مِنْ هَوْلٍ بِوَقْفَتِهِ

This is the intercessor for a conclusive judgment when
everyone is bewildered by the terrors of his situation

نَأْتِي لِآدَمَ لَا يَقْبَلْ مَقَالَتَنَا

يَقُولُ نَفْسِى وَ عِصْيَانِى بِجَنَّتِهِ

We will come to Ādam, who will not accept our plea,
saying, 'Myself, and my rebellion in His Garden'

نَأْتِي لِنُوحٍ فَلَا يَرْضَى يُذَكِّرُنَا

إِغْرَاقَ قَوْمٍ لَهُ وَفْقاً لِدَعْوَتِهِ

We will come to Nūḥ, who will not consent—reminding us
of the drowning of his people on the basis of his supplication

نَأْتِي الخَلِيلَ فَلَا يَرْضَى وَ يَذْكُرُ مَا

قَدْ كَانَ مِنْ قَوْلِهِ أُخْتِي لِزَوْجَتِهِ

We will come to al-Khalīl[49], who will not accept—mentioning
the words, 'Sister,' he once uttered about his wife

نَأْتِي لِمُوْسَى فَلَا يَرْضَى وَ يَذْكُرُ مَا

قَدْ كَانَ مِنْ قَتْلِهِ نَفْساً بِوَكْزَتِهِ

We will come to Mūsā, who will not approve—mentioning
his killing a soul at one time with his fist

نَأْتِي لِعِيْسَى فَلَا يَرْضَى وَ يُرْشِدُنَا

إِلَى النَّبِيِّ فَيَا بُشْرَى لِأُمَّتِهِ

We will come to ʿIsā, who will not agree—guiding us
to the Prophet, such good news to his nation!

فَنَأْتِهِ زُمَراً نَسْعَى فَيَقْبَلُنَا

وَ يَنْجَلِي كَرْبُنَا مِنْ بَعْدِ سَجْدَتِهِ

We will rush to him in groups, and he will welcome us,
our distress will vanish after his prostration

يَا مُنْكِراً لِأُمُورٍ نَحْنُ نَفْعَلُهَا

يَوْمَ القِيَامَةِ فِي أَهْوَالِ شِدَّتِهِ

O rejector of matters we engage in
on the Day of Standing amid calamitous horrors

49 Sayyiduna Ibrāhīm ﷺ

إِنَّ التَّوَسُّلَ يَوْمَ الحَشْرِ نَفْعَلُهُ
وَ الْيَوْمَ نُنْكِرُهُ مِنْ بَعْدِ شُهْرَتِهِ

We use him as a means on the Day of Resurrection,
yet today we deny that, despite its renown.

أَ يُشْرِكُ العَبْدُ بَعْدَ البَعْثِ وَ اعَجَباً
أَمْ يَجْهَلُ العَبْدُ تَوْحِيداً بِمَوْتَتِهِ

Does the slave commit *shirk* after resurrection? Amazing!
Or is a slave unaware of tawḥīd when death befalls him?

يَا نَايِرَ الوَجْهِ يَا مَنْ قَوْلُهُ حِكَمٌ
فَكَمْ شَفَى أُمَماً تِرْيَاقُ حِكْمَتِهِ

O one whose face is light, O one whose speech is wisdom!
How many nations were cured by the antidote of his wisdom

يَا صَادِقَ الوَعْدِ يَا مَنْ طَابَ مَبْدَؤُهُ
وَ طَابَ آخِرُهُ أَكْرِمْ بِسِيرَتِهِ

O fulfiller of promises, O one of pleasant origin
O one whose end is pleasant! Honor his biography

يَا طَيِّبَ الأَصْلِ يَا مَنْ كَانَ مَوْلِدُهُ
فَخْراً لِمَكَّةَ إِذْ فَازَتْ بِطَلْعَتِهِ

O one of pleasant stock, O one whose birth was
a source of pride for Makka, since triumph is by his emergence

إِنَّ المَدِينَةَ قَدْ حَازَتْ فَضَايِلَ لَا
تُحْصَى بِدَفْنِ نَبِيٍّ بَعْدَ هِجْرَتِهِ

Madīna earned merits which no one can
count by the Prophet being buried [there] after his migration

يَا لَيْتَنِي كُنْتُ مِمَنْ كَانَ يَخْدُمُهُ
يَا لَيْتَنِي كُنْتُ خَدَّاماً لِبَغْلَتِهِ

O how I wish I was one of those serving him!
O how I wish I was the one looking after his mule!

أَوْ خَادِماً لِنِعَالٍ كَانَ يَحْمِلُهَا
ذَاكَ الصَّحَابِي ابْنُ مَسْعُودٍ بِهِمَّتِهِ

Or taking care of the sandals he used to carry!
That [blessed task] fell on Ibn Mas'ūd the Companion, by his yearning

أَهْوَى لِمَنْ فَرَضَ المَوْلَى مَحَبَّتَهُ
وَ خَصَّهُ بِأُمُورٍ فِي رِسَالَتِهِ

I love the one the Master commanded us to love,
singling him out for matters in his Message

لَهُ الغَنَايِمُ قَدْ حَلَّتْ وَ قَدْ طَهُرَتْ
لَهُ الأَرَاضِي وَ قَدْ نَارَتْ بِبِعْثَتِهِ

His are the spoils, lawful and pure
his are the lands, lighted by his advent

مَنْ فَاقَ شَمْسَ الضُّحَى وَ الشَّمْسُ قَدْ غَرَبَتْ
وَ ضَوْءُ أَحْمَدَ وَقَّادٌ بِجَبْهَتِهِ

The one who surpassed the midday sun and at sunset
and the light of Aḥmad is radiant on his forehead

وَ نُورُ وَجْهِكَ مَحْبُوبٌ وَ قَدْ سُكِبَتْ
لَهُ المَدَامِعُ حُبًّا فِي مَلَاحَتِهِ

The light on your face is beloved, and it has poured forth
because of it, tears out of love for its beauty

الشَّمْسُ تَحْجُبُهَا الأَسْتَارُ إِنْ سُتِرَتْ
وَ ضَوْءُ نُورِكَ لَمْ يُحْجَبْ لِرِفْعَتِهِ

The sun is screened by curtains when it is veiled,
but the light of your face is unveiled in its loftiness

أَنْوَارُ دِينِكَ لِلأَعْمَى لَقَدْ ظَهَرَتْ
وَ الشَّمْسُ تَخْفَى وَ لَمْ تُدْرَكْ لِمُقْلَتِهِ

The lights of your Dīn to the blind man are plain,
while the sun is hidden, and his eye cannot comprehend it

اللَّيْلُ زَالَ ضِيَاءُ الشَّمْسِ فَانْسَتَرَتْ
وَ ضَوْءُ وَجْهِكَ لَمْ يُحْجَبْ بِظُلْمَتِهِ

At night, the light of the sun departs concealed,
but the light of your face is not veiled by darkness

الْبَدْرُ يُحْجَبُ إِنْ جَاءَ النَّهَارُ وَ قَدْ
يَزْدَادُ وَجْهُكَ تَنْوِيراً بِضَحْوَتِهِ

When morning comes, the full moon is shrouded,
but your face grows in light as the day progresses

قَدْ تُكْرَهُ الشَّمْسُ إِنْ زَادَتْ حَرَارَتُهَا
وَ يَضْعُفُ الْبَدْرُ أَحْيَاناً بِدَوْرَتِهِ

The sun might be loathed when its heat increases
and the full moon sometimes weakens in its orbit

الْجِذْعُ أَنَّ لِطَهَ عِنْدَ مِنْبَرِهِ
وَ جَاءَ يَسْعَى وَ يَبْكِي مِنْ مَحَبَّتِهِ

The stump moaned to Ṭāhā at his minbar
so he rushed to it while it was weeping out of love for him

وَ الشَّمْسُ رُدَّتْ لَهُ مِنْ بَعْدِ مَا غَرَبَتْ
وَ زَالَ عَنَّا الْعَنَا مِنْ حُسْنِ دَعْوَتِهِ

The sun was restored for him after setting
and hardship from us removed by the excellence of his supplication

الْبَدْرُ شُقَّ لَهُ نِصْفَيْنِ إِذْ طَلَبَتْ
مِنْهُ الأَعَادِي انْشِقَاقاً نَحْوَ مَكَّتِهِ

The moon was split for him in half when requested
by the enemies split up towards Makka

شَكَى البَعِيرُ لَهُ الأَحْزَانَ فَانْدَفَعَتْ
كَمَا شَكَا رَجُلٌ قَحْطاً بِبَلْدَتِهِ

The camel complained to him of grief that was dissolved
likewise, a man lamented a drought that struck his country

سُبْحَانَ رَبِّي لَقَدْ أَعْطَاكَ مَنْزِلَةً
لَمْ يُعْطِهَا أَحَداً يَا بَابَ رَحْمَتِهِ

Glory to my Lord who gifted you a status
he gave to no one else, O door to His Mercy!

يَا بَحْرَ عِلْمٍ رَوَى الأَقْوَامَ حِكْمَتُهُ
يَا غَيْثُ أَغْنَى فَقِيراً بَعْدَ جَوْعَتِهِ

O sea of knowledge whose wisdom quenched the people!
O rain enriching a poor man previously hungry!

آوَاكَ رَبِّي بِإِحْسَانٍ فَكُنْتَ لَهُ
عَبْداً شَكُوراً تُنَادِينَا لِطَاعَتِهِ

My Lord sheltered you in goodness, so you were for Him
a grateful slave calling us to His obedience

أَغْنَاكَ رَبِّي بِمَالٍ كُنْتَ تُنْفِقُهُ
نَحْوَ الكِرَامِ وَ لَمْ تَبْخَلْ بِخَيْرَتِهِ

My Lord made you rich with wealth which you expended
on the noble, without withholding the choicest part of it

هَدَاكَ رَبِّي إِلَى سِرٍّ فَجِئْتَ بِمَا
قَدْ أَعْجَزَ الخَصْمِ إِتْيَانٌ بِسُورَتِهِ

My Lord guided you to a secret, so you came with
that which the opponent could not bring a Sūra like it

أَعْطَاكَ رَبُّكَ قُرآناً وَ مَنْزِلَةً
تَعْلُو المَنَازِلَ فِي الدُّنْيَا وَ جَنَّتِهِ

Your Lord gave you a Qur'ān and a rank
topping all ranks in this world and in His Paradise

شُرِحْتَ صَدْراً بِهِ الأَسْرَارُ قَدْ جُمِعَتْ
رُفِعَتْ ذِكْراً وَ قَدْ فُزْنَا بِرِفْعَتِهِ

Your heart was expanded, with secrets which are gathered in it
your mention is elevated, and by its highness we are victorious

هَذَا النَّبِيُّ أَبُو الزَّهْرَاءِ فَاطِمَةٍ
طُوْبَى لِمَنْ جَاءَهُ يَسْعَى لِزَوْرَتِهِ

This Prophet is the father of Fātima, the Resplendent
blessedness to the one who hastens to pay a visit

سَارَ الحَجِيْجُ لِطَهَ خَيْرِ مُحْتَرَمِ
يَمْشُونَ هَرْوَلَةً شَوْقاً لِطَيْبَتِهِ

The pilgrims set out for Ṭāhā, the most respected soul,
speeding up their pace, longing for his Ṭāyba

يَا رَبِّ بِالمُصْطَفَى عَفْواً وَ مَغْفِرَةً
وَ وَفِّقِ العَبْدَ أَنْ يَسْعَى لِرَوْضَتِهِ

Lord, by the Chosen one, grant pardon and forgiveness
and give success to the slave to speedily arrive to his Rawḍa

عَبْدٌ حَقِيرٌ مُحِبٌّ لِلَّذِى شَهِدَتْ
لَهُ الأَعَادِى بِصِدْقٍ فِى بِدَايَتِهِ

A lowly slave loving the one whose truthfulness
enemies themselves acknowledged at the outset

هُوَ الأَمِينُ هُوَ المَأْمُونُ كَمْ سَهِرَتْ
عَيْنَاهُ تَبْكِي وَ كَمْ بَلَّتْ لِلِحْيَتِهِ

He is the trustworthy and the trusted; How often
has his sleepless eyes shed tears; How often his beard became wet [with tears]

يَا رَبِّ بِالمُصْطَفَى عَفْواً وَ مَرْحَمَةً
وَ وَفِّقِ الكُلَّ لِلتَّقْوَى لِشِرْعَتِهِ

O Lord, by the Chosen one, grant pardon and mercy
and give success to everyone towards taqwā and his Sharī῾a

أَنَا الفَقِيرُ أَنَا المَسْكِينُ فِى وَجَلٍ
يَا رَبِّ عَفْواً وَ نَوِّرْنِى بِنَظْرَتِهِ

I am the poor, I am the destitute in dread
O Lord, Your pardon, and by his gaze enlighten me!

إِنْ تَاقَ قَلْبُكَ لِلْمُخْتَارِ فِي شَغَفِ

فَزُرْ حُسَيْناً فَهَذَا إِبْنُ بَضْعَتِهِ

If your heart yearns for the Chosen one passionately,
visit Ḥusayn, for this son is a part of him

ثُمَّ الرِّضَا عَنْ أَبِي بَكْرٍ خَلِيفَتِهِ

مَنْ كَانَ صَاحِبَهُ فِي غَارِ هِجْرَتِهِ

Then satisfaction with Abū Bakr, his successor,
who was his companion in the cave during his Hijra

كَذَا الرِّضَا عَنْ أَبِي حَفْصٍ أَمِيرِ هُدًى

قَدْ كَانَ يَهْدِي بِرِفْقٍ أَوْ بِشِدَّتِهِ

Likewise, satisfaction with Abū Ḥafṣ[50], Amīr of guidance
he guided with compassion or severity

ثُمَّ الرِّضَا عَنْ مُنِيرِ الوَجْهِ سَيِّدِنَا

عُثْمَانَ مَنْ نَالَ أَجْراً بَعْدَ بَلْوَتِهِ

Then satisfaction with the illumined face, our master
'Uthmān, who obtained reward after affliction

كَذَا عَلِيٍّ أَبِي السِّبْطَيْنِ مَنْ فَنِيَتْ

بِهِ جُيُوشٌ لِكُفْرٍ عِنْدَ كَرَّتِهِ

Likewise, with ʿAlī, the father of the two scions, at whose hands
Armies of kufr were wiped out when they attacked him

---

[50] Sayyiduna ʿUmar b. al-Khaṭṭāb

كَذَا الرِّضَا عَنْ أَمِيرِ المُؤْمِنِينَ أَبِي
مُحَمَّدِ الحَسَنِ المُصْلِحْ بِإِمْرَتِهِ

Likewise, satisfaction with the Amīr of the faithful Abū
Muḥammad, al-Ḥasan, the reconciler through his leadership

كَذَا الرِّضَا عَنْ حُسَيْنٍ إِبْنِ فَاطِمَةٍ
نِعْمَ الشَّهِيدُ لَهُ نُورٌ بِجَنَّتِهِ

Likewise, satisfaction with Ḥusayn, the son of Fātima
how excellent of a martyr! He has a light in his Garden

كَذَا الرِّضَا مِنْ إِلَهِي نَحْوَ فَاطِمَةٍ
بِنْتُ النَّبِيِّ لَهَا فَخْرٌ بِنِسْبَتِهِ

Likewise, satisfaction from my God with Fātima too,
daughter of the Prophet, pride of his lineage

يَا بِنْتَ طَهَ وَ يَا زَوْجَ الإِمَامِ عَلِيِّ
يَا بِنْتَ طَهَ الَّتِي فَازَتْ بِبُشْرَتِهِ

O daughter of ṬāHā, O wife of Imām ʿAlī
O daughter of ṬāHā, who received his glad tidings

أَفَاطِمُ أَنْتِ فِي الجَنَّاتِ خَالِدَةٌ
بُشْرَى النَّبِيِّ وَ قَدْ فُزْنَا بِزَوْرَتِهِ

Dear Fātima, you will be in the Gardens eternally
glad tidings of the Prophet, we were successful in visiting him

ثُمَّ الرِّضَا مِنْ إِلَهِي نَحْوَ زَيْنَبَ مَنْ
نَالَتْ مِنَ اللَّهِ سِرًّا فِي عِبَادَتِهِ

Then satisfaction from my God with Zaynab, who
obtained from Allah a secret in His worship

يَا أُمَّ هَاشِمِ يَا بِنْتَ البَتُولِ وَ يَا
بِنْتَ الإِمَامِ فَدُلِّينِي لِحَضْرَتِهِ

O mother of Hāshim, O daughter of the Chaste, and O
daughter of the Imām, guide me to his presence

ثُمَّ الرِّضَا عَنْ عَلِيٍّ زَيْنِ حَضْرَتِنَا
إِمَامُ عِلْمٍ صَدُوقٌ فِي مَقَالَتِهِ

Then satisfaction with our master ʿAlī Zayn,
Imām of knowledge, veracious in his sayings

وَ أُخْتِهِ مَنْ لَهَا فَضْلٌ فَكَمْ سَجَدَتْ
لِلَّهِ فِي لَيْلِهَا شُكْراً لِنِعْمَتِهِ

With his sister, virtuous. How often she prostrated
to Allah at night, thankful for His blessings

كَذَا نَفِيسَتُنَا مَنْ كَانَ مَجْلِسُهَا
فَهْمَ الكِتَابِ وَ ذِكْراً فِي تِلَاوَتِهِ

Likewise, with our Nafīsa, whose circle of learning was
understanding the Book, and deep remembrance in its recitation

كَذَا سُكَيْنَةُ تَتْلُوهُمْ وَ عَايِشَةٌ
وَ أَنْوَرٌ وَ لِمَنْ حَلُّوا بِسَاحَتِهِ

Likewise, Sukayna who follows them, and ʾĀ'isha
Then Anwar and one by whose courtyard they alighted

كَذَا رُقَيَّةُ وَ الأَشْرَاف قَاطَبَةً
مِنْ آلِ أَحْمَدَ مَنْ فَازُوا بِنُصْرَتِهِ

Likewise, with Ruqayya, with all the noble descendants
from the family of Aḥmad, by his support they were successful

يَا رَبِّ إِرْضَ عَنِ الأَزْوَاجِ قَاطَبَةً
أَزْوَاجِ طَهَ وَ أَوْلَادٍ وَ عِتْرَتِهِ

O Lord, be pleased with all the wives,
the wives of ṬāHā, his children and his 'Itra[51]

بِالمُصْطَفَى وَ بِآلٍ مِنْ سُلَالَتِهِ
شَرَّفْتَ قَدْرَهُمُ مِنْ تَحْتِ بُرْدَتِهِ

By the Chosen one, and his family of descendants
whose rank was honored from beneath his cloak

يَا آلَ طَهَ مُحِبٌّ جَاءَ زَايِرَكُمْ
يَبْكِي إِلَيْكُمْ وَ يَشْكُو ظُلْمَ شَهْوَتِهِ

O family of ṬāHā, a lover came to visit you
crying to you, lamenting the darkness of his passions

---

51 Progeny in general, often a specific reference to ʿAlī, Fāṭima, Ḥasan and Ḥusayn ﷺ

هَذَا المُحِبُّ إِلَيْكُمْ جَاءَ يَمْدَحُكُمْ

يَرْجُو بِفَضْلِ الرِّضَا تَنْوِيرَ مُقْلَتِهِ

To you, this lover has come singing your praises
hoping by gracious satisfaction that his eyes are brightened

أَنْتُمْ كِرَامٌ وَ عُرْبٌ وَ المُحِبُّ أَتَى

ضَيْفاً إِلَيْكُمْ فَقُومُوا فِي ضِيَافَتِهِ

You are generous, eloquent, and the lover came
as your guest, so be to him a host

يَا آلَ أَحْمَدَ يَا مَنْ جَاءَ مَدْحُكُمُ

مِنَ الإِلَهِ وَ تَبْشِيرٌ بِجَنَّتِهِ

O family of Aḥmad, O those whose praises came
from the Divine, and glad tidings of His Garden

يَا أَكْرَمَ العُرْبِ قَدْ جَاءَ المُحِبُّ لَكُمْ

لَا يَأْتِهِ فَشَلٌ فِي دَارِ غُرْبَتِهِ

O noblest Arabs, the lover has come to you
disappointment does not come to him in the abode of estrangement

حَاشَاكُمُ أَنْ تَرُدُّوا العَبْدَ فِي وَجَلٍ

وَ قَدْ أَتَاكُمْ بِشَوْقٍ مِنْ مَحَبَّتِهِ

God forbid that you turn away the slave in dread
while he has come to you with longings out of his love

يَبْكِي الفُؤَادُ إِذَا فَارَقْتُ مَشْهَدَكُمْ
وَ العَيْنُ تَدْمَعُ حُزْناً عِنْدَ فُرْقَتِهِ

The heart cries when I part from your resting places
and the eye weeps out of sadness at the time of separation

يَا سَادَةً يَا كِرَامَ القَوْمِ مَادِحُكُمْ
بِالبَابِ يَرْجُو لِأَنْوَارٍ بِمَدْحَتِهِ

O masters, O nobles of the people, your panegyrist
is at your door, hoping for lights from his praise

إِنَّ الشَّفِيعَ لَنَا فِي الحَشْرِ جَدُّكُمُ
قَدْ فَاقَ كُلَّ نَبِيٍّ فِي شَفَاعَتِهِ

Our intercessor when revived is your Grandfather
he excelled every prophet in his intercession

أَنَا الفَقِيرُ أَنَا المِسْكِينُ جِئْتُكُمُ
أَنَا الذَّلِيلُ أَنَا البَاكِي بِعَبْرَتِهِ

I, the one in need, the destitute, have come to you
I am the abased, I am the weeper shedding tears

ثُمَّ الصَّلَاةُ عَلَى المُخْتَارِ سَيِّدِنَا
مَنْ جَاءَ يَهْدِي الوَرَى أَنْوَارَ حِكْمَتِهِ

Then the prayer on the Chosen one, our master
on him who guides creatures to the lights of his wisdom

وَ الآلِ وَ الصَّحْبِ وَ التَّسْلِيمُ يَتْبَعُهَا

أَزْكَى صَلَاةٍ بِأَنْوَارٍ بِرَوْضَتِهِ

On the family, companions, and peace, followed by
the purest prayer with lights in his Rawḍa

-17-

## God is Pleased

يَا رَبِّ صَلِّ عَلَى النَّبِي

مَنْ جَاءَنَا بِرِسَالَةِ

O Lord, send prayers on the Prophet
he who came to us with a message

يَرْضَى الإِلَهُ عَنِ الَّتِي

أَضْحَتْ بِأَقْصَى مَكَّةِ

The Divine is pleased with the one who
was from the farthest side of Makka

زَوْجُ النَّبِيِّ مُحَمَّدٍ

أَكْرِمْ بِهَا بِخَدِيجَةِ

The wife of the Prophet Muḥammad
honor her, honor Khadīja

سَلِّمْ عَلَيْهَا كُلَّمَا

زُرْتَ الْحَجُونَ بِرَحْمَةِ

Greet her whenever
you visit al-Ḥajūn[52] with mercy

سَادَتْ عَلَى كُلِّ النِّسَا

ءِ بِفَضْلِهَا فِي مَكَّةِ

She prevailed over all women
by her virtue in Makka

أُمُّ البَتُولِ وَ نَسْلُهَا

فَاقَ الوَرَى بِمَزِيَّةِ

Mother of the Chaste, and her progeny
excelled all mankind by their merit (birthright)

بِالمُصْطَفَى سَادُوا وَ قَدْ

أَضْحَوْا كَشَمْسٍ ظَهِيرَةِ

By virtue of the Chosen one, they were masters,
becoming like the midday sun

قَدْ بَشَّرَتْ خَيْرَ الوَرَى

بِفَضَايِلٍ وَ سَجِيَّةِ

She gave the best of creation glad tidings
of virtues and good nature

52 The name of a mountain in Makka.

فِي بَيْتِهَا قَدْ جَاءَهُ
وَحْيُ الهُدَى بِرِسَالَةِ

In her house, on him descended
the Revelation of guidance with a Message

قُمْ يَا مُحَمَّدُ مُنْذِراً
كَبِّرْ إِلَهَ الأُمَّةِ

'Rise, O Muḥammad, as warner,
magnify the God of your nation'

قَالَ الحَبِيبُ لَهَا اسْمَعِي
إِنِّي أُرَى فِي رَوْعَةِ

the Beloved told her, 'Listen!'
'I am alarmed.'

قَالَتْ لَهُ كَلاَّ فَلَا
تَحْزَنْ بِأَيِّ فَجِيعَةِ

She told him, 'No way,'
'Do not grieve over any calamity

أَفْعَالُكَ الحُسْنَى الَّتِي
عَمَّتْ لِكُلِّ قَبِيلَةِ

Your actions are beautiful, which
encompasses every tribe

أَرْضَيْتَ رَبَّكَ دَايِماً

أَبْشِرْ بِكُلِّ سَكِينَةِ

You please your Lord invariably
rejoice with full serenity

مُسْتَبْشِراً وَ مُكَبِّراً

وَ مُؤَيَّداً بِالنُّصْرَةِ

Delighted, magnifying Allah,
supported by victorious help

وَ اذْكُرْ كَلَاماً قَالَهُ

مَنْ جِئْتَهُ بِالشُّورَةِ

Remember the words uttered
by the one you have consulted

إِذْ قَالَ إِنَّكَ مُرْسَلٌ

وَ مُبْشَّرٌ بِالبِعْثَةِ

When he said you were a Messenger
blessed with good news of Prophethood,

وَ مُبَشَّرٌ بِرِسَالَةِ

تُدْعَى بِهَا لِلهِجْرَةِ

Blessed with good news of Messengership
for which you will be called to migration'

رِضْوَانَكَ اللَّهُمَّ يَا
رَبَّ الوَرَى لِخَدِيجَةِ

Your Pleasure, O Allah
for Khadīja, O Lord of creation!

فِي قَصْرِهَا وَ نَعِيمِهَا
تَلْقَى الهَنَا بِالنِّعْمَةِ

In her palace and bliss
she receives happiness with blessings

مَنْ زَارَهَا لِلمُصْطَفَى
فَلَهُ دُخُولُ الجَنَّةِ

Whoever visits her for the sake of the Chosen one
is entitled to enter the Garden

إِذْ أَنَّهَا زَوْجٌ لَهُ
مَعْرُوفَةٌ بِالحِكْمَةِ

She is in fact his wife
renowned for her wisdom

وَ يَدُ النَّبِيِّ لِقَبْرِهَا
وَضَعَتْ تُرَابَ الرَّوْضَةِ

The hand of the Prophet, for her tomb
laid the soil of the Meadow

هَذَا التُّرَابُ مُبَارَكٌ

بِمُحَمَّدٍ وَ بِقَبْضَةِ

This soil is blessed
through Muḥammad and a handclasp

أَبْشِرْ إِذَا مَا زُرْتَهَا

لِلَّهِ خَيْرَ زِيَارَةِ

Rejoice when you visit her
for the sake of Allah, the best visit

وَ إِذَا أَتَيْتَ مَقَامَهَا

تَدْعُو لَهَا بِالرَّحْمَةِ

And when you come to her maqam,
supplicate for her to receive mercy

يَا رَبِّ فَارْضَ عَنِ الَّتِي

قَدْ أَنْجَبَتْ لِلبَضْعَةِ

O Lord, be pleased with her who
gave birth to one who is a part [of him],

بِنْتِ النَّبِيِّ مُحَمَّدٍ

أَكْرِمْ بِهَا مِنْ دَوْحَةِ

The daughter of Prophet Muḥammad
honor her for her family tree

مَنْ أَنْجَبَتْ رَيْحَانَتَيْـ

ـهِ وَ شُرِّفَتْ بِالهِجْرَةِ

She who gave birth to his two sweet basils
and was ennobled by migration

مَعَ أَحْمَدٍ لِمَدِينَةٍ

تُدْعَى لَدَيْهِ بِطَيْبَةِ

with Aḥmad to al-Madīna,
named due to him: Ṭāyba[53]

ثُمَّ الصَّلَاةُ عَلَى الَّذِى

قَدْ جَاءَنَا بِالحِكْمَةِ

Then the prayer of blessings on the one
who brought to us the wisdom

وَ الآلِ وَ الأَصْحَابِ مَا

سَارَ الحَجِيجُ بِزَوْرَةِ

On his Family and Companions, so long
as the pilgrims set out on a visit

53 Pleasant.

## -18-

## Hasten Towards Them

وَ صَلَاةُ اللّٰهِ تَحِيَّتُهُ

لِلهَادِى النَّاسِ إِلَى النَّهَجِ

Blessings of Allah and His greetings
to the guide for humanity, to the way

عَجِّلْ بِالسَّعْيِ لِنَحْوِهِمِ

تَلْقَ الرِّضْوَانَ وَ تَبْتَهِجِ

Hasten with effort towards them:
you will receive pleasure and joy

هُمْ أَهْلُ البَيْتِ أَئِمَّتُنَا

فِي الخُلْدِ لَهُمْ أَعْلَى الدَّرَجِ

They are the household, our leaders
eternally. Theirs is the loftiest course

سَلِّمْ تَسْلَمْ وَ انْظُرْ عَجَباً

تِلْكَ الأَنْوَارُ مِنَ الفَرَجِ

Greet them, and be safe, and look at a wonder:
those lights issuing forth from relief

وَ اشْرَبْ وَ اطْرَبْ وَ انْشَقْ عَطِراً

قَدْ فَاقَ شَذَاهُ عَلَى الأَرَجِ

Drink and enjoy, and smell the perfume
whose fragrance has outstripped musk

قَوْمٌ سَادُوا فِي الخُلْدِ عَلَى

أَهْلِ الجَنَّاتِ أُوْلَى السُّرُجِ

A people who prevailed eternally over
the inhabitants of the Gardens, possessors of lamps

وَ لَهُمْ جَاهٌ وَ بِجَدِّهِمُ

يَنْجُو مَنْ زَارَ فَذَاكَ نُجِي

Theirs is a glorious rank and by their Grandfather
they save those who visit them, so be saved!

أَبْشِرْ إِنْ جِئْتَ لِدَارِهِمُ

قَدْ فُزْتَ سَرِيعاً بِالفَرَجِ

Rejoice if you come to their abode
you quickly earn relief

سَادُوا الأَقْطَابَ لَهُمْ شَرَفُ

يُضْوِى كَالشَّمْسِ لَدَى المُهَجِ

They excelled the poles; for them is all nobility
illuminating like the sun for those possessing hearts

إِذْهَبْ بِاللَّيْلِ لِرَوْضَتِهِمْ

أَقْدِمْ أَسْرِعْ بِالحُبِّ وَجِى

Go at night to their meadow,
be bold. Hasten with love and come

أَخْلِصْ لِلَّهِ بِزَوْرَتِهِمْ

أَخْلِصْ فِي السَّيْرِ بِلَا عِوَجِ

Be sincere to Allah when visiting
be sincere in your travel, with no straying

رَاقِبْ لِلنَّفْسِ وَ شَهْوَتِهَا

إِيَّاكَ تُصَاحِبُ لِلهَمَجِ

Be mindful of the self and its passions
beware of the company of riffraff

إِعْرَفْ قَدْرَ الأَحْبَابِ وَ كُنْ

عِنْدَ الأَحْبَابِ أُوْلَى الدَّرَجِ

Learn the rank of the lovers and be
amid the lovers, those of the way

وَ اسْمَعْ مِنْهُمْ مَا تَسْمَعُهُ
إِنْ كُنْتَ سَمِيعاً وَ ابْتَهِجِ

Hear from them what you hear
if an ear you lend, and be glad

فَهُنَاكَ لِرُوْحِكَ أَسْرَارٌ
تَخْفَى الأَسْرَارُ عَلَى السَّمِجِ

There are secrets for your soul,
but secrets elude the loathsome

وَ لِأَهْلِ الحُبِّ مُعَتَّقَةٌ
كَأْسُ الأَسْرَارِ بِلَا وَهَجِ

For devotees of love, a matured wine:
a cup of secrets without blaze

فَاشْرَبْ مَا دُمْتَ مُحِبَّهُمُ
كَأْساً تَنْهَاكَ عَنِ العِوَجِ

Drink, so long as you love them,
a goblet preventing you from crookedness

وَ اسْمَعْ أَقْوَالَ مُحِبِّهِمِ
كَالشَّهْدِ بِهِ أَقْوَى الحُجَجِ

Listen to the speech of their lover
as if honey spilling the clearest proof

وَ دَعِ الإِنْكَارَ لِمُنْكِرِهِ
عَبْدٌ مَحْرُومٌ فِي لُجَجِ

Leave refutation to the refuter:
a slave deprived in stubbornness

لَوْ شَاهَدَ نُورَ أَحِبَّتِنَا
مَا أَنْكَرَ إِنْكَارَ اللَّجَجِ

If he witnessed the light of our beloveds
he would not deny as the obstinate do,

مَا قَالَ مَقَالَةَ ذِى جَهْلٍ
مَا قَالَ مَقَالَةَ ذِى عِوَجِ

He would not utter the words of the ignorant,
he would not utter the words of deviancy

وَ صَلَاةُ اللَّهِ تَحِيَّتُهُ
لِلهَادِى النَّاسِ إِلَى النَّهَجِ

Prayers of Allah and His greetings
to the guide for humanity, to the way

وَ الآلِ جَمِيعاً سَادَتِنَا
أَهْلُ التَّوْفِيقِ إِلَى البَلَجِ

To his whole family, our masters
the people of Divine success to happiness,

مَا صَالِحُ يَتْلُو أَمْدَاحاً
تُضْوِي لَيْلاً مِثْلَ السُّرُجِ

So long as Ṣāliḥ recites eulogies
lighting up at night as if they were lamps

-19-

## O Father of the Resplendent!

أَبَا الزَّهْرَاءِ يَا نِعْمَ المُرَجَّى
وَ يَا نِعْمَ المُؤَمَّلُ يَا مُؤَيَّدْ

O Father of the Resplendent, O lovely source of hope!
O lovely prop of the hopeful, O supported one!

عَلَيْكَ اللّٰهُ رَبُّ الخَلْقِ صَلَّى
كَذَا الأَمْلَاكُ صَلُّوا عَلَى مُحَمَّدْ

On you, Allah, the Lord of creation, sends prayers,
likewise the angels send prayers on Muḥammad

وَ يَوْمَ الحَشْرِ مَلْجَا الخَلْقِ طُرًّا
جَمِيعُ الخَلْقِ تَأْتِي إِلَى مُحَمَّدْ

On the Day of Resurrection, he is for everyone a shelter
all creatures will come to Muḥammad

رَأَى مَوْلَاهُ رَبَّ العَرْشِ حَقًّا
وَ مَا نَظَرَ الإِلَهَ سِوَى مُحَمَّدْ

He saw his Master, the Lord of the Throne, in reality!
None saw the Divine except Muḥammad

شَفِيعُ الخَلْقِ مَقْبُولٌ مُشَفَّعْ
بِيَوْمِ الحَشْرِ شَافِعُنَا مُحَمَّدْ

Intercessor for creation, whose intercession is accepted
on the Day of Resurrection, our intercessor is Muḥammad

وَ فِي التَّوْرَاةِ وَ الإِنْجِيلِ يَتْلَى
ثَنَاءُ اللّٰهِ جَاءَ عَلَى مُحَمَّدْ

In the Torah and Gospel is recited
the praise of Allah on Muḥammad

كَذَا القُرْآنُ فِيهِ ثَنَاءُ رَبِّي
عَلَى المُخْتَارِ سَيِّدِنَا مُحَمَّدْ

Likewise in the Qur'ān is the praise of my Lord
on the Chosen one, our master Muḥammad

إِمَامُ المُرْسَلِينَ لَهُ المَزَايَا
جَمِيعُ الرُّسْلِ صَلَّى بِهِمْ مُحَمَّدْ

Leader of the Messengers, he enjoys prerogatives
he led all Prophets in prayer, Muḥammad

وَ لا يَأْتِي نَبِيٌّ بَعْدَ طَهَ
خِتَامُ الرُّسْلِ سَيِّدُنَا مُحَمَّدْ

No Prophet will come after Ṭāhā,
the Seal of Messengers, our master Muḥammad

وَ إِنْ ضَاقَتْ بِكَ الأَحْوَالُ يَوْماً
فَبِالأَسْحَارِ صَلِّ عَلَى مُحَمَّدْ

And if the situations of the day cause you difficulty,
spend the pre-dawn hours sending prayers on Muḥammad

يُصَلِّي اللّٰهُ رَبُّ العَرْشِ عَشْراً
عَلَى عَبْدٍ يُصَلِّي عَلَى مُحَمَّدْ

Allah sends ten prayers
on the slave who sends one prayer on Muḥammad

وَ فِي مِائَةٍ يُصَلِّي اللّٰهُ أَلْفاً
فَعَجِّلْ بِالصَّلَاةِ عَلَى مُحَمَّدْ

Allah sends one thousand prayers for every hundred
hasten then to send prayers on Muḥammad!

وَ لا تَتْرُكْ رَسُولَ اللّٰهِ يَوْماً
فَمَا أَحْلَى الصَّلَاةَ عَلَى مُحَمَّدْ

Do not neglect the Messenger of Allah for a single day,
how sweet indeed is the prayer on Muḥammad!

شِفَاءٌ لِلقُلُوبِ لَهَا ضِيَاءٌ
وَ نُورٌ مُسْتَمَدٌّ مِنْ مُحَمَّدْ

A cure for the hearts, regaled with brightness
and a light derived from Muḥammad

بِهَا يُسْرٌ وَ تَفْرِيجٌ لِكَرْبٍ
لِمَنْ أَهْدَى الصَّلَاةَ عَلَى مُحَمَّدْ

By it, there is ease and relief from distress
for the one who gifts prayers on Muḥammad

بِهَا الأَسْرَارُ وَ الأَنْوَارُ تَتْرَى
تَنَوَّرْ بِالصَّلَاةِ عَلَى مُحَمَّدْ

By it, secrets and lights,
be illumined by the prayer on Muḥammad

وَ أَفْضَلُهَا إِذَا مَا كُنْتَ يَوْماً
بِرَوْضَتِهِ تُصَلِّ عَلَى مُحَمَّدْ

The best of it will be when one day you are
in his Rawḍa sending prayers on Muḥammad

تُصَلِّ بِاشْتِيَاقٍ فِي مَقَامٍ
عَظِيمِ الشَّأْنِ يَسْمَعُهَا مُحَمَّدْ

You send prayers with a longing at the maqam,
a sublime affair, and it is heard by Muḥammad

وَ لَاحَ النُّورُ تُبْصِرُهُ مُضِيئاً
وَ فَاحَ الطِّيبُ مِسْكاً مِنْ مُحَمَّدْ

Light shines, and you will perceive it gleaming
and perfume exudes as musk from Muḥammad

وَ تِلْكَ مَزِيَّةٌ حَصَلَتْ لِقَوْمٍ
تَرَاهُمْ نَاظِرِينَ إِلَىٰ مُحَمَّدْ

That is a privilege accorded to people
whom you see gazing at Muḥammad

وَ جَاءُوا نَحْوَهُ وَ لَهُمْ سَلَامٌ
فَرَدَّ عَلَيْهِمْ طَهَ مُحَمَّدْ

They came to him with a salutation
and got a reply from ṬāHā, Muḥammad

فَيَا سَعْدَ الَّذِى قَدْ جَاءَ يَوْماً
وَ قَدْ أَهْدَى السَّلَامَ عَلَى مُحَمَّدْ

How fortunate is he who one day came
and conveyed his greeting to Muḥammad

تَقِيٌّ بَلْ سَعِيدٌ مُسْتَجَابٌ
وَ يَوْمَ الحَشْرِ شَافِعُهُ مُحَمَّدْ

God fearing, nay, blissful, his pleas accepted
and on the Day of Gathering his intercessor is Muḥammad

كَلَامِي لِلَّذِي قَدْ زَارَ يَوْماً
حَبِيبَ اللَّهِ هَادِينَا مُحَمَّدْ

My speech is for him who one day visits
the beloved of Allah, our guide Muḥammad

فَذَاكَ لَهُ مِنَ الأَذْوَاقِ سِرٌّ
إِذَا بِالحُبِّ جَاءَ إِلَىٰ مُحَمَّدْ

This person has a secret associated with tasting
when he comes with love to Muḥammad

فَكَأْسُ الحُبِّ يُسْقَاهَا مُحِبٌّ
بِجَوْفِ اللَّيْلِ صَلَّى عَلَى مُحَمَّدْ

The cup of love is passed around to a lover
who in the heart of the night sends prayers on Muḥammad

وَ عِنْدَ المُصْطَفَى ظَهَرَتْ مَزَايَا
لِأَرْبَابِ الصَّلَاةِ عَلَى مُحَمَّدْ

Privileges with the Chosen one have emerged
for devotees of the prayer upon Muḥammad

فَيَا مَنْ عِنْدَهُ سِرٌّ تَبَدَّى
مِنَ المُخْتَارِ سَيِّدِنَا مُحَمَّدْ

How blessed is the one to whom the secret appears
from the Chosen one, our master Muḥammad

تَعَلَّمْ حِفْظَ سِرِّكَ يَا أَخَانَا
وَ لا تَنْسَ الصَّلَاةَ عَلَى مُحَمَّدْ

Learn to guard your secret, O brother
and do not forget the prayer on Muḥammad

إِذَا مَا شِئْتَ أَنْ تَحْظَى قَرِيباً
بِفَتْحِ اللَّهِ صَلِّ عَلَى مُحَمَّدْ

If you wish to be granted soon
an opening from Allah, send prayers on Muḥammad

وَ تَفْسِيرٌ وَ عِلْمٌ ذُو مَعَانِي
لِمَنْ ذَكَرُوا الصَّلَاةَ عَلَى مُحَمَّدْ

An explanation and meaningful knowledge
for those who remember prayers on Muḥammad

وَ رِزْقُ اللَّهِ أَوْسَعُهُ تَبَدَّى
لِأَرْبَابِ الصَّلَاةِ عَلَى مُحَمَّدْ

The provision of Allah, the most expansive of it manifests
to devotees of the prayer on Muḥammad

وَ تَيْسِيرُ الأُمورِ لِمَنْ يُصَلِّي
عَلَى المُخْتَارِ سَيِّدِنَا مُحَمَّدْ

Affairs are facilitated for whoever sends prayers
on the Chosen one, our master Muḥammad

شِفَاءٌ لِلمَرِيضِ كَذَا دَوَاءٌ
صَلَاةُ العَاشِقِينَ عَلَى مُحَمَّدْ

Healing for the sick, likewise a cure,
the prayer of the ardent lovers on Muḥammad

وَ جَاءَتْكَ المَكَارِمُ مِنْ كَرِيمٍ
إِذَا يَوْماً تُصَلِّي عَلَى مُحَمَّدْ

From the Noble one, noble traits will lodge in you
if one day you send prayers on Muḥammad

وَ رَدَّ اللَّهُ أَضْرَارَ الأَعَادِي
عَنِ الأَخْيَارِ صَلُّوا عَلَى مُحَمَّدْ

Allah repels harm from enemies
from the choicest of people who send prayers on Muḥammad

تَوَجَّهْ إِنْ أَرَدْتَ قَضَاءَ دَيْنٍ
إِلَى كَنْزِ الصَّلَاةِ عَلَى مُحَمَّدْ

If you want debts fulfilled, direct yourself
to the treasure of the prayer upon Muḥammad

تَجِدْ فَرَجاً قَرِيباً يَا أَخَانَا
بِجَاهِ نَبِيِّنَا طَهَ مُحَمَّدْ

You will find quick relief, O brother
by the rank of our Prophet ṬāHā, Muḥammad

عَلَيْهِ اللّٰهُ صَلّٰى كُلَّ حِينٍ
صَلَاةَ الأَوَّلِينَ عَلَى مُحَمَّدْ

On him, Allah sends prayers all the time,
the prayers of the early ones upon Muḥammad

عَلَيْهِ اللّٰهُ سَلَّمَ مَا تَبَدَّتْ
رَوَاحِلُ زَائِرِينَ لَدَى مُحَمَّدْ

To him, Allah sends salutations of peace as long as there appears
conveyances of those paying visit to Muḥammad

وَ آلِ البَيْتِ سَادَاتٍ كِرَامٍ
لَهُمْ شَرَفُ القَرَابَةِ مِنْ مُحَمَّدْ

And on the household, noble masters
blessed by nobility of kinship with Muḥammad

عَلَى الصَّحْبِ الكِرَامِ رِضَاءُ رَبِّي
كَذَاكَ رِضَاءُ سَيِّدِنَا مُحَمَّدْ

Along with the noble Companions is the pleasure of my Lord
likewise the pleasure of our master, Muḥammad

عَنِ الصِّدِّيقِ وَ الفَارُوقِ أَيْضاً
وَ عُثْمَانَ الحَيِيّ لَدَى مُحَمَّدْ

And upon the Ṣiddīq and the Fārūq as well
and with ʿUthmān the modest before Muḥammad,

أَبِى الحَسَنَيْنِ سَيِّدِنَا عَلِيٍّ
بِنِسْبَتِهِ القَرِيبِ إِلَىٰ مُحَمَّدْ

The father of the two Ḥasans, our master ʿAlī
by his close ties of kinship with Muḥammad

وَ أَصْحَابٍ كِرَامٍ يَوْمَ بَدْرٍ
تَرَاهُمْ مُحْدِقِينَ عَلَى مُحَمَّدْ

With the noble Companions of the Day of Badr
whom you see as his guards, surrounding Muḥammad

وَ أَصْحَابٍ كِرَامٍ يَوْمَ أُحْدٍ
تَرَاهُمْ وَاقِفِينَ لَدَى مُحَمَّدْ

With the noble Companions of the Day of Uḥud
whom you see standing beside Muḥammad

وَ مَنْ هَجَرُوا الدِّيَارُ إِلَىٰ دِيَارٍ
بِهَا المُخْتَارُ سَيِّدُنَا مُحَمَّدْ

With those who migrated from lands to lands
with them the Chosen one, our master Muḥammad

وَ أَنْصَارُ المَدِينَةِ هُمْ كِرَامٌ
لَقَدْ سَعِدُوا بِسَيِّدِنَا مُحَمَّدْ

With the Madīnan Helpers, a noble folk
who were blessed by the company of our master Muḥammad

رِضَاءُ اللَّهِ مَقْبُولٌ عَلَيْهِمْ
لِأَجْلِ المُصْطَفى طَهَ مُحَمَّدْ

The pleasure of Allah and acceptance is upon them
for the sake of the Chosen one, ṬāHā, Muḥammad

وَ جَعْفَرُ صَادِقٌ جَدِّى وَ إِنِّي
بِنِسْبَتِهِ يُوَافِقُنِي مُحَمَّدْ

Ja'far al-Ṣādiq is my ancestor and so
by his relation he is favorable to me, Muḥammad

وَ جَدِّى الجَعْفَرِيُّ لَهُ دَوِيٌّ
يُرَدِّدُ لِلصَّلَاةِ عَلَى مُحَمَّدْ

My grandfather al-Ja'farī reverberates
with the constant repetition of the prayer upon Muḥammad

وَ يَحْفَظُ لِلكِتَابِ كِتَابَ رَبِّي
وَ عَلَّمَهُ وَ كَمْ لِلخَلْقِ أَرْشَدْ

He knows by heart the Book, the Book of my Lord
he taught it, and how many creatures he has guided

وَ يَحْفَظُ لِلدَّلَايِلِ حِفْظَ صَدْرٍ
وَ يَقْرَؤُهَا وَ يَسْمَعُهُ مُحَمَّدْ

He knows by heart the "Dalā'il al-Khayrāt"
and recites it while Muḥammad listens

عَلَى شَيْخِي هُوَ ابْنُ ادْرِيسَ أَحْمَدْ
لَهُ نَسَبٌ إِلَىٰ طَهَ مُحَمَّدْ

To our shaykh, Aḥmad Ibn Idrīs
linked by lineage to ṬāHā, Muḥammad

وَ بَحْرٌ فِي العُلُومِ لَهُ دُرُوسٌ
وَ يُسْنِدُ لِلحَدِيثِ إِلَىٰ مُحَمَّدْ

An ocean of erudition, giving lessons,
with chains in Ḥadith all the way back to Muḥammad

دَعَاكَ الجَعْفَرِيُّ أَيَا كَرِيمُ
يُرِيدُ زِيَارَةَ الهَادِي مُحَمَّدْ

al-Jaʿfarī supplicates to you, 'O Generous!'
desiring to visit the guide, Muḥammad

وَ يَسْبَحُ فِي بِحَارِ النُّورِ سَبْحاً
يُشَاهِدُ حَضْرَةَ الهَادِي مُحَمَّدْ

He swims in seas of light with vigor
he witnesses the presence of the guide, Muḥammad

وَ يَنْفَعُ لِلْعِبَادِ بِعِلْمِ شَرْعٍ
بِتَفْسِيرِ حَدِيثٍ عَنْ مُحَمَّدْ

He benefits the slaves by the knowledge of the Sharīʾa
by explaining the Ḥadith from Muḥammad

وَ يُكْسَى هَيْبَةً مِنْ فَضْلِ رَبِّي
تُكَلِلُ بِالصَّلَاةِ عَلَى مُحَمَّدْ

He is clothed with awe from the bounty of my Lord
crowned by the prayer on Muḥammad

وَ مَنْ يَلْقَاهُ يُبْصِرُهُ ضِيَاءً
يَشِعُّ عَلَيْهِ نُورٌ مِنْ مُحَمَّدْ

Whoever meets him, perceives him as glow
on him is a light radiating from Muḥammad

يَدُومُ عَلَيْهِ فَضْلُكَ يَا إِلَهِي
وَ رِضْوَانٌ مِنَ الهَادِي مُحَمَّدْ

May Your favor on him abide, O my God
along with a pleasure from the guide, Muḥammad

-20-

## The Pure Blessings

صَلَوَاتٌ طَيِّبَاتٌ

لِلْحَبِيبْ مَوْلَاى مُحَمَّدْ

Pure blessings
for the Beloved, mawlay[54] Muḥammad

فَاحَ طِيبُ المِسْكِ فَاحَا

هَيَّجَ القَلْبَ فَبَاحَا

The fragrance of musk scents the air,
exciting the heart, its love it declared

حَرَّكَ الطَّرْفَ فَنَاحَا

مِنْ غَرَامٍ فِي مُحَمَّدْ

Moving the eyes to shed their tears,
out of deep love of Muḥammad

54 Mawlay: my master, Mawlana: our master.

طَيْبَةُ المُخْتَارِ طَيْبَةْ

حُبُّهَا يَا نَاسُ قُرْبَةْ

The Ṭāyba[55] of the Chosen One
loving it, O people, is nearness!

لَيْتَنَا يَا قَوْمُ صُحْبَةْ

عِنْدَ مَوْلَانَا مُحَمَّدْ

How I wish, O people, we were all in company,
near mawlana Muḥammad

لَيْتَنَا نَلْقَى الحَبِيبَا

حُبُّهُ أَضْحَى عَجِيبَا

How I wish we would meet the Beloved,
his love has become truly wondrous

لَيْتَنَا نَسْعَى قَرِيبَا

لِلْحَبِيبْ مَوْلَاىْ مُحَمَّدْ

How I wish we would travel soon,
to the Beloved, mawlay Muḥammad

رَوْضَةٌ تَعْلُو الْعَوَالِي

حُبُّهَا فِي الْقَلْبِ غَالِي

A Rawḍa elevated in exaltedness
love of it in the heart is precious

55 al-Madina

هَيَّمَتْ كُلَّ الرِّجَالِ
عَاشِقِينْ مَوْلَاىْ مُحَمَّدْ

It captivates all men [making them]
passionate lovers of mawlay Muḥammad

نُورُهَا نُورٌ بَدِيعُ
قَدْرُهَا قَدْرٌ رَفِيعُ

Its light is a wondrous light,
Its worth is a worth so high!

سَاكِنٌ فِيهَا الشَّفِيعُ
أَكْرَمُ الرُّسْلِ مُحَمَّدْ

In it lives the intercessor,
the most noble of messengers, Muḥammad

مَنْ أَتَاهَا لَيْسَ يَشْقَى
كُلَّ خَيْرٍ سَوْفَ يَلْقَى

He who comes to it will not suffer,
every goodness he will meet

دَارُ خَيْرِ الخَلْقِ حَقًّا
الحَبِيبْ مَوْلَاىْ مُحَمَّدْ

The house of the best of creation, in truth
the Beloved, mawlay Muḥammad

مَنْ بِهِ الْكَوْنُ تَشَرَّف

وَإِلَيْهِ اللَّهُ أَتْحَفْ

The one by which existence is honored
and Allah gave as a gift

إِنَّ رَبِّي قَدْ تَلَطَّفْ

مِنْ قَدِيمٍ بِمُحَمَّدْ

Indeed my Lord has been gentle
from pre-eternity with Muḥammad

أَفْضَلُ الخَلْقِ جَمِيعًا

يَأْتِي فِي يَوْمٍ شَفِيعًا

The best of all creation
he comes on the day as an intercessor

يُكْشَفُ الكَرْبُ سَرِيعًا

بِسُجُودٍ مِنْ مُحَمَّدْ

Difficulties are removed swiftly
by the prostrations of Muḥammad

هَنِّئُونَا يَا أَفَاضِلْ

إِنْ ذَهَبْنَا فِي القَوَافِلْ

The notables congratulate us
when we come in caravans

وَنَزَلْنَا فِي المَرَاحِلْ

قَاصِدِينْ مَوْلَاىْ مُحَمَّدْ

We stop at the waystations
intending mawlay Muḥammad

وَرَأَيْنَاهُ جِهَارَا

نُورُهُ فَاقَ النَّهَارَا

And we saw him appearing clearly
his light surpasses the light of day

قَلْبُ أَهْلِ الحُبِّ طَارَا

لِلْحَبِيبْ مَوْلَاىْ مُحَمَّدْ

The hearts of the people of love, flew
to the Beloved, mawlay Muḥammad

إِنْ وَصَلْتُمْ بِاللَّيَالِي

فَانْظُرُوا بَدْرَ المَجَالِي

When you arrive in the nights
look at the full moon of manifestations

فَاقَ دُرًّا فِي اللَّآلى

الحَبِيبْ مَوْلَاىْ مُحَمَّدْ

Surpassing pearls in their lustre
the Beloved, mawlay Muḥammad

وَادْخُلُوا بَابَ السَّلَامِ

وَاذْهَبُوا نَحْوَ المَقَامِ

Enter the gate of Peace[56]
and go toward the maqam

بِأَمَانٍ وَاحْتِرَام

زَايِرِينْ مَوْلَاىْ مُحَمَّدْ

With security and respect
visiting mawlay Muḥammad

وَاسْكُبُوا دَمْعَ الْقُلُوبِ

وَاشْرَبُوا مَاءَ الْغُيُوبِ

Pour out the tears of the hearts,
and drink the water of the unseen

لَا تُفَكِّرْ فِي الذُّنُوبِ

شَافِعٌ فِيهَا مُحَمَّدْ

Do not think of your sins,
for he will intercede in them, Muḥammad

وَتَرَنَّمْ بِالْمَدَايِحْ

نُورُ خَيْرِ الْخَلْقِ لَايِحْ

Sing the panegyrics!
The light of the best of creation shines

56 One of the oldest gates of Masjid al-Nabawī.

طِيبُهُ يَا نَاسُ فَايِحْ

الْحَبِيبْ مَوْلَايْ مُحَمَّدْ

His fragrance, O man, exudes
the Beloved, mawlay Muḥammad

عِنْدَ رُؤْيَاهُ يَرَانَا

عِنْدَمَا زُرْنَا المَكَانَا

When we see him there, he sees us,
when we visit that blessed place -

رَوْضَةٌ فِيهَا هُدَانَا

الْحَبِيبْ مَوْلَايْ مُحَمَّدْ

The Rawḍa in which is our guide,
the Beloved, mawlay Muḥammad

يَوْمُ عِيدٍ عِنْدَ قَلْبِي

حِيْنَمَا لَاقَيْتُ حِبِّي

A day of Eid it is for my heart
when I meet my beloved

خَيْرُ خَلْقِ اللَّهِ طِبِّي

الْحَبِيبْ مَوْلَايْ مُحَمَّدْ

The best of creation, my medicine,
the Beloved, mawlay Muḥammad

ثُمَّ قُولُوا إِنْ وَصَلْتُمْ
وَأَتَيْتُمْ وَدَخَلْتُمْ

Then say, when you arrive
come and enter

وَذَهَبْتُمْ وَنَظَرْتُمْ
لِلْحَبِيبْ مَوْلَاىْ مُحَمَّدْ

Go and look
at the Beloved, mawlay Muḥammad

يَا رَسُولَ اللّٰهِ أَنْتَ
قَبْلَ خَلْقِ الخَلْقِ كُنْتَ

O Messenger of Allah, you
were before the creation of the creation

مِنْ ضِيَاءٍ قَدْ خُلِقْتَ
عِنْدَ رَبِّي يَا مُحَمَّدْ

From light you were created,
with my Lord, O Muḥammad

قَدْ أَتَيْنَا فِي جَمَاعَهْ
نَرْتَجِى مِنْكَ الشَّفَاعَةْ

We have come in a congregation,
seeking your intercession

شَرْعُكَ المَحْبُوبُ طَاعَةْ

قَدْ أَطَعْنَا يَا مُحَمَّدْ

Your beloved law is about obedience,
we have obeyed, O Muḥammad!

رَبَّنَا إِنَّا أَتَيْنَا

مِنْ بِعَادٍ وَسَعَيْنَا

Our Lord we have come,
from far away we travelled

رَبَّنَا فَانْظُرْ إِلَيْنَا

بِالْحَبِيبْ مَوْلَاىْ مُحَمَّدْ

Our Lord we ask you to look at us,
by the Beloved, mawlay Muḥammad!

صَلَوَاتٌ طَيِّبَاتٌ

زَاكِيَاتٌ نَامِيَاتٌ

Pure blessings
increasing and growing

غَالِيَاتٌ دَايِمَاتٌ

لِلْحَبِيبْ مَوْلَاىْ مُحَمَّدْ

Precious and perpetual
for the beloved, mawlay Muḥammad

نَاظِمُ الدُّرِّ المُحَرَّرْ
شَيْخُنَا مِنْ آلِ جَعْفَرْ

The composer of these written pearls,
our shaykh[57] from the family of Jaʿfar—

رَاجِى فَضْلاً مِنْكَ أَكْبَرْ
بِالْحَبِيبْ مَوْلَاىْ مُحَمَّدْ

is asking you for Your grace most great,
by the Beloved, mawlay Muḥammad!

57 Originally says 'Ṣāliḥ' instead of 'Our shaykh'.

www.ingramcontent.com/pod-product-compliance
Lightning Source LLC
Chambersburg PA
CBHW030257100526
44590CB00012B/430